1/24

STRAND PRICE
$ 5.00

D1376633

Edwardian Excursions

BY THE SAME AUTHOR

Godliness and Good Learning
A History of Wellington College
The Parting of Friends
Two Classes of Men
On the Edge of Paradise

Edwardian Excursions

FROM THE DIARIES OF A.C.BENSON
1898–1904

Selected, edited
and introduced by
DAVID NEWSOME

JOHN MURRAY

© Introduction, and introductions
to Diary extracts, David Newsome 1981

© Extracts from A C Benson's Diaries,
The Master and Fellows
of Magdalene College, Cambridge 1981

First published 1981
by John Murray (Publishers) Ltd
50 Albemarle Street, London W1X 4BD

All rights reserved
Unauthorised duplication
contravenes applicable laws

Printed in Great Britain by
The Pitman Press, Bath

British Library Cataloguing in Publication Data

Benson, A C
Edwardian excursions.
1. Benson, A C – Diaries
2. Authors, English – 19th century – Diaries
I. Title   II. Newsome, David
828'.8'09   PR4099.B5Z
ISBN 0–7195–3769–X

Contents

Illustrations

◇

ILLUSTRATION SOURCES

1 from *The Diary of Arthur Christopher Benson* edited by Percy Lubbock, 1927; 2 courtesy of Humberside County Record Office; 3 copyright: Gwynedd Archives Services; 4 and 6, *Illustrated London News*; 5 *The Studio*, Winter 1909; 7 from *Highways and Byways in Oxford and the Cotswolds* by H. A. Evans, 1905; 8 from the Sir Benjamin Stone Collection, courtesy of the Birmingham Reference Library; 9 and 10 from *Arthur James Balfour* by Blanche Dugdale, 1936.

Acknowledgements

⬦

For allowing me to produce a companion volume to *On The Edge of Paradise: A. C. Benson, the Diarist*, consisting of edited extracts from the first sixty volumes of Arthur Benson's Diaries, I am indebted yet again to the Master and Fellows of Magdalene College, Cambridge, in whose custody these diaries have been kept since Benson's death in 1925. Both Dr Walter Hamilton (formerly Master of Magdalene) and Mr Robert Latham (Pepys Librarian) have helped me with advice; and Mr Roger Hudson of John Murrays deserves my very special thanks for his work in tracking down period photographs of some of the places here described.

To my wife, Joan, I am especially grateful for accompanying me on several expeditions during the Summer of 1980, retracing some of the walks and rides that Arthur Benson undertook at the turn of the century, and also for her help in the compilation of the index.

David Newsome

Introduction

◇

Praised be thou, O my Lord, of our brother the *Bicycle*,
Who holdeth his breath when he runneth,
And is very swift and cheerful and unwearied, and silent.
He beareth us hither and thither very patiently,
And when he is sick he doth not complain.

So, in the summer of 1902, Arthur Benson paid his tribute to
the bicycle, by his own individual addition to St Francis'
Hymn to the Sun. 'Hither and Thither' his bicycle certainly
took him in the years of his travels, the seven years between
1898 and 1904, when he was a housemaster at Eton in his late
thirties. He had given up Alpine climbing, following an
accident in 1896. He was only once thereafter, before his
death in 1925, to take a holiday abroad again, and then only
in reluctant response to the advice of his doctor. His passion
now became the discovery of his own country, going off
when he could in each of his vacations, sometimes with a
close friend as companion, to explore Wales, Fenland, the
Norfolk Broads, the Cotswolds – on the whole places that
offered not the overpowering dramatic effects of mighty
mountains and awesome crags, but the more delicate
treasures, hidden because subdued, off the beaten track in
rural England, relatively unvisited and therefore unspoiled.

This book tells not only of the excursions which he liked
best, to holiday haunts and distant, lonely retreats. During
these same years Arthur Benson made some memorable visits
to interesting people or to important events; all of them
recorded with extraordinary fidelity in the massive diary
which he began to compile during the summer of 1897: to
Westminster Abbey for the funeral of Mr Gladstone and for
the coronation of Edward VII (he took his bicycle to the

I

latter, but had a servant to collect it at Waterloo and take charge of it until he needed it); to Dublin to stay with the Viceroy of Ireland, the Earl of Cadogan (no bicycle there; he travelled everywhere in state); to visit Algernon Swinburne at Putney, when he cycled all the way from Eton; on a holiday in Scotland with his friends, the Donaldsons, to lunch with the Prime Minister at Whittingehame, the Balfour family home. They all cycled in a party together.

Time was when Arthur abandoned his bicycle for a motor-car (his first long ride in one is described in the account of his holidays on the Norfolk Broads). This was in the days when he had become a relatively rich man, after the publication of *The Upton Letters* and *From a College Window* and, as Fellow of Magdalene College, Cambridge, he sought for further independence by taking a house at Haddenham in the Fens. This period of his life lies outside the limits of this book and was in itself productive of dozens of volumes of diary which supplied their own collection of fresh vignettes and descriptions of the late Edwardian period. Even so, in his heart, Arthur always looked back wistfully to the days of his cycling feats – the joyous independence of two wheels, going fast enough to cover thirty or forty miles a day, but slowly enough to notice the little things – the churches, the houses, the tiny dramas of life in a cottage garden or in a village street – as you passed.

The whole of this book is a series of period pieces – self-contained narratives or descriptions taken from the most remarkable diary that has ever been preserved; remarkable partly for its unique length (180 volumes in all, covering the years 1897 to 1925), and also for the richness of its detail, written by an acknowledged master of the diarist's art. Only recently has this intriguing source, in the possession of Magdalene College, Cambridge, become available for use, because Arthur Benson – as Master of Magdalene – forbad (excepting only his close friend, Percy Lubbock, who was allowed to publish a highly-diluted selection) any inspection

of its contents for fifty years after his death. Before returning
to the evocations of Edwardian England, as illustrated by the
selection of writings here, it may be helpful to supply a brief
word about the diarist and his life.

Even when Arthur Benson had compiled only a hundred
pages of his record, one discerning critic, who was allowed to
see what he had written, made a judgement on its quality.
Henry James was the favoured recipient of Arthur's tentative
efforts, and he firmly approved. What he actually said had
the characteristic note of Jamesian sententiousness. He congratulated Arthur on producing 'a series of data on the life of
a young Englishman of great endowments, character and
position at the end of the nineteenth century'.

Arthur conceded that this was a little extravagant, but
typical of Henry James' generosity. He recognised that as the
eldest surviving son of Edward White Benson, Archbishop
of Canterbury (who had died in 1896), he occupied a
dignified position in society, which in some ways he rather
more resented than respected because of the expectations
which that eminent start in life imposed upon him; and
although an Eton housemaster mingled frequently with the
great and occupied a position and status which might well
open up more glorious posts in the future, he was more
conscious, at this stage of his life, of the drudgery of the
responsibility which denied him the opportunity to indulge
his real passion and ambition – to become a prominent
literary figure. Nor would he accept Henry James' estimate
of his endowments and character. His diary abounds in
passages of genuinely harsh self-analysis, accusing himself of
timidity and ineffectiveness; and – as for his endowments – he
felt that these he had largely squandered, so that he was
highly dubious about his prospects for the future. 'I am very
busy', he wrote in the same month that Henry James saw fit

to compliment him, '. . . God knows I am not complacent. I have plenty of unqualified faults; and I am nobody in this busy place except a pleasant, sociable person, rather reclusive but amiable when extracted. I have no influence or weight. My business capacities are mistrusted; my accuracy doubted; my originative powers discredited; my *auctoritas* non-existent. I do not mind this and it keeps me humble, I hope.'

The fascination of reading a great diary is that not only does one not know what is going to happen next, but the writer himself does not know either. When Henry James made his judgement on Arthur's promise as a diarist, neither he nor Arthur could have had the faintest conception of what the experiment would lead to, let alone what Arthur's life held in store. All that he saw was an early fragment of a huge collection which, by the time of Arthur's death, had grown into a chronicle of nearly five million words. As a record of a man's private thoughts and hopes, agonies, frustrations and aspirations it is unique; but, more than that, its 'data' (to use Henry James' word) of the life, conventions and *mores* of English society between the years 1897 and 1925, admittedly as viewed by one particularly perceptive pair of eyes, constituted an exceptionally informative and detailed back-cloth to the social, political and cultural history of these times.

In this respect, Henry James judged correctly. Even in the short extract that he read, he could discern that Arthur Benson had the endowments of the natural *diarist*. He combined the instincts of the *voyeur* with the talent of the artist in words. He was fascinated by other people, their quirks and idiosyncrasies, the little things that made them different, the gestures and expressions which gave them vitality, the personal absurdities that made them both laughable and lovable. He had a photographic eye which could recall minutiae of natural effects and the tiniest details of buildings and a craftsman's designs. All through his life he had been blessed (or cursed, as he sometimes felt) with an essentially spectatorial disposition. Even as a little boy his chief delight had been simply looking at things, and reflecting upon them and trying to find the words to describe them. When he became a figure of consequence – as Head of a Cambridge House, or as a recognised literary personality among the giants of his day – his chief occupation, while attending Committee meetings or supposedly important discussions or ceremonies, was to examine his colleagues carefully, to cherish secret mirth at their self-importance, and to savour in anticipation the description of the scene that would be chronicled later in the diary. For much as he wrote – and he published over sixty books in the course of his career – the literary exercise that gave him most satisfaction was the private record he was keeping in his journals, which his contemporaries would never see but which his posterity would – one day – savour and enjoy.

It helped, of course, to occupy a suitable vantage-point from which to observe the doings and posturings of interesting people. Here, again, Henry James was correct in recognising the advantage of Arthur Benson's position. If it was true in 1897, it remained so throughout his life. Already Arthur had established himself as a prominent figure within various different, but equally intriguing, circles. He was thoroughly at home within the world of the Anglican Church, being the son of an Archbishop and linked by ties of close friendship to the families of the Taits and the Davidsons. He was given an entrée at Court, through his ability to produce odes and lyrics for royal occasions almost to order ('Land of Hope and Glory' was just one of these, thrown off in the course of an idle hour). He had been a King's Scholar at Eton and served as a master there for twenty years. As Housemaster to the young Duke of Albany and the sons of the Earl of Cadogan, Lord St Germans, Lord Northampton and the Duke of Westminster, he was brought quite naturally, if a little self-consciously, into the circle of the late Victorian and Edwardian aristocracy. When he left Eton for

Introduction

Cambridge, as Fellow of Magdalene, in 1904, he found himself again in the Eton circle at King's, and through these friendships he was admitted, before long, to the inner circle of Cambridge worthies. Even as a young man he had come to the notice of Henry James and Edmund Gosse, and although he was never really part of the London literary world, he enjoyed his position on the periphery, meeting at one time or another all the great luminaries of that circle, from Browning and Swinburne to the later generation of Hardy, Belloc, Chesterton and Wells.

Given this vantage-point, he indulged unashamedly his temperamental disposition and natural skills – to observe, to describe, to caricature, to mock; without exception to cast over all a naturally disrespectful eye and to translate the image without delay into graphic description and pungent, caustic prose.

So vast is this collection of diaries that to publish them *in extenso* would be an impossible undertaking. They certainly afford material for a biography, if proper allowance is made for the subjectivity of the source. It was actually in no spirit of self-inflation or unpleasing self-esteem that Arthur himself wanted his diary to be used in this way. He believed in all sincerity that the most interesting biographies of all were those of really rather ordinary people, who aspired to no particular eminence in their own achievements, but who left behind them a sufficient body of honest reflections to cast light, from their individual standpoint, upon some particular corner of the history of their times. Such a biography has been recently attempted in my book, *On the Edge of Paradise: A. C. Benson the Diarist*.

But to leave the matter at that would be a gross disservice to Arthur Benson, whose diary contains many more treasures than revelations about himself, his friendships, his everyday doings and concerns. The record embraces not only the reflections of a *journal intime*; it is also something of a literary portfolio – a sort of verbal sketchbook, with long descriptive passages recalling walks and expeditions, notable visits and memorable occasions, compiled sometimes with a view to possible publication at some later date; little essays composed round vignettes of contemporary life, as much an exercise in the art of writing as *aide-memoires* to evoke scenes and conversations which had caused pleasure or amusement.

In a biography, many of these episodes – especially the holiday chronicles – are too static to warrant more than a passing comment. To do justice to the wealth of material that Arthur recorded, then, it has seemed desirable to produce a selection of some of the most interesting and attractive of these self-contained pieces, choosing not only those of specific historical or literary significance, but also those which are purely period-pieces, evocative of an age – although not all that long past – sufficiently far back in memory to exude the quaintness and the charm of a family-album of sepia-tinted photographs found in some forgotten corner of attic, cubby-hole or loft.

No one consciously composes a period piece, because the writer has no means of knowing what will appear quaint or odd to a later generation. Arthur described his walks and expeditions in the hope that some future reader would follow in his footsteps and share something of the same joys and pleasures he himself had felt. Our first thought will surely be – how little of what he describes has survived. The people seen and memorialised in some charming vignette are now long dead; the country-inns, serving ginger-beer to thirsty cyclists, and the tea-parlours for hikers and the luncheon-hampers for travellers by train, even the steam-trains themselves, are all relics of the past or have changed their custom and their clientele. The eau-de-Cologne machine at Weighton station is no more – indeed, very few of the stations themselves have survived; and there is no longer a Viceroy in Dublin.

Introduction

Most of the natural features, however, are timeless. Cader Idris still stands, and the view is much the same as ever it was. Ranworth Church, with its painted screen, is still to be visited, and the sedge still blows in a high wind to delight the ear. The absurd ecclesiastical monuments and stained-glass windows which caused Arthur and Herbert Tatham such merriment are still (for the most part) untouched. I have little doubt that with the help of an ordnance-survey map the farm called Fairholme, on the way to Swine (where Arthur and Lionel Ford lost themselves on a hot and drowsy afternoon) could still be found, with the paths and tracks not much Changed. Certainly the Lygon Arms at Broadway, where Arthur wrote the first of the *Upton Letters*, looks very much the same as it did in 1904.

To retrace these walks would be sentimental journeys, no doubt. The descriptions, however, are refreshingly free from the sentimental and the mawkish. Arthur himself admitted that when he came to write for publication, he could not somehow refrain from assuming his 'company manners'. The prose became affected and strained. So frequently did he write in the vein of serene and leisurely avuncularity that he came in his later books time and time again to parody himself. In his diary, however, he wrote rapidly and unselfconsciously. On occasions he would try out a purple patch, when endeavouring to recall some particularly sublime or rhapsodic moment; but, on the whole, the diary reads as Arthur talked, not as he composed for his avid and somewhat undiscriminating reading-public.

The self-contained extracts given here have been subjected to a minimum of editing. A few spellings have been corrected; there has been some repunctuation (Arthur tended to use dashes for sentence-breaks). Some very local and irrelevant comments have been omitted. Since Arthur himself never revised his diaries or corrected anything he had written, the fluency of the original text is quite remarkable. Each extract has been annotated, firstly, by the inclusion of

Introduction

brief introductions, in order to set the piece in context, and secondly by notes identifying some of the characters mentioned and some of the more enigmatic and obscure allusions. On the whole, passages have been selected which do not appear in Percy Lubbock's earlier book, conceived on an entirely different principle. The notable exception is the account of Arthur's visit to Algernon Swinburne in 1903, which is so remarkable that it ought to be printed in an unexpurgated form.

One final word about the designation 'Edwardian' in the title. A few of the earlier pieces fall within the period 1898–1900 before Edward VII actually became King (in February 1901). This is rather more than mere editorial licence. The last decade of Queen Victoria's reign up to the gathering of the storm clouds which heralded the outbreak of European war were quintessentially the Edwardian years. As the nineteenth century drew to its close, a new age was being born, marked by the advent of the new aristocracy of wealth, the creed of secularism and the widespread mood of emancipation. Arthur was too much the son of his archiepiscopal father to be able to accept all these changes with equanimity. He felt a deep loyalty to the Queen which he could never transfer to her pleasure-loving son. Temperamentally a Victorian, however, he did not embark upon his continuous chronicle until the twilight of the old Queen's reign. All these pieces are set against a background of Edwardianism; and the journeys, scenes and visits here described are therefore, without exception, the record or logbook of Edwardian excursions.

I

He pays his respects to a
great statesman at Westminster Abbey:
Gladstone's funeral, 28 May 1898

W. E. Gladstone died on 19 May 1898. In August of the previous year, Arthur Benson had visited Hawarden and attended a family dinner-party, sitting on Gladstone's right. Much of the conversation that ensued, recorded faithfully in his diary, Arthur later recounted in his compendium of Eton worthies, *Fasti Etonenses*. The bond between the Gladstone and Benson families had become quite close during the statesman's last years. It was, after all, Gladstone who raised Edward White Benson to the primacy in December 1882. Thereafter a deep mutual respect and affection developed between the two men. Indeed, Archbishop Benson died at Hawarden, at a service in Hawarden Parish Church, when he was staying with the Gladstones just after a very exhausting tour of Ireland in October 1896.

It was obvious, then, that the Benson family would be placed in a position of honour at the burial of the G.O.M. in Westminster Abbey. Not for the last time in his life did Arthur inadvertently leave things to the last minute and discover that he had misunderstood the arrangements for procuring his ticket of admission. A similar mistake was made in November 1902, at the first performance of the Coronation Ode at the Queen's Hall, conducted by the composer (Edward Elgar). On that occasion, Arthur – as author of the Ode (in which his most famous lyric, 'Land of Hope and Glory', occurs) – assumed that he needed no ticket and found that he had to queue to purchase one at the last minute.

Arthur obtained a seat in the Abbey, if not the place reserved for him; and he witnessed exactly the sort of service or ceremony that he most delighted to record. After the funeral, he dined with A. C. Ainger, his Eton colleague, and found that Lewis ('Loulou') Harcourt, the eldest son of Sir William Harcourt (successively Home Secretary and Chancellor of the Exchequer in Gladstone's four administrations) was also a guest. Inevitably the conversation centred on the events of the day, and the description by Loulou Harcourt of Gladstone's last days during his illness forms a fitting epilogue to this account.

On Friday I received a letter from Herbert Gladstone inviting me to the funeral – I had not thought of applying – and telling me to call at Cleveland Square for the ticket. I went up with Jack Lyttelton[1] after early school and was at C.S. by 9.30. The Gladstones all gone, and certain envelopes on the table, but none for me or Jack. One, addressed to the Captain of Eton School and Captain of the Oppidans I nearly bagged, and found out after that it *did* contain my ticket.

We drove on, but having no tickets were stopped by Marlborough House and had to walk. Pushed through the police cordon by saying 'The Deanery' (where Mamma was staying). The crowd gathering, but rather thinly, I thought; the police in great force. At Deanery, found a polite butler. Dean gone into Abbey and all the party gone in; could not send in or admit me. I went in despair to Cloister Gate. Inspector could do nothing. While we debated, Warre[2] passed and Mrs Alfred Lyttelton[3] and

---

[1] The eldest of the Lyttelton boys in Arthur's House. His grandmother (Mary Glynne) was the younger sister of Mrs Gladstone (Catherine Glynne).
[2] Edmond Warre, Head Master of Eton.
[3] Edith Balfour, the daughter of A. J. Balfour.

others. At last caught the Precentor and explained my case. He got a message taken to the Dean, and meantime we were shown up to the roof of the Jerusalem Chamber, where we had a good view of the crowd. Every window and balcony now full and the number below increasing.

Presently the Dean[4] came out. I found him in the hall in cassock with the ribbon and badge of the Bath round his neck. His pale sharp features – long silken hair very picturesque, to say nothing of his thin voice and little sharp glances. He threw up his hands: 'I have no authority. The Abbey is taken from me. Of *course* you must have a place, and Mr Lyttelton too. Come with me.' He led us past all the inspectors – the whole place was closely guarded, people assembling as thick as bees but with good wide spaces left – and marched on right up close to the Gladstones. Then he stated my case and left me saying with a smile 'That's all I can do!' I told my case to a rather rude Seneschal, named Williamson, filled with temporary importance. 'No use – no seats – can do nothing without a ticket.' Presently he asked my name. I told him. He said 'The late Archbishop's son?' I said 'Yes'. He then appeared more satisfied and became polite. He said 'Why not go in with the House of Lords?' At last he said, 'Well, it *is* very awkward. There is no doubt a place here for you, only we don't know which it is. Why not sit *there*?' and he showed me a place. I walked across to Lady Cobham to ask whether she knew where my ticket was. She wanted to clear a place for me with them, but I went back. Mrs Henry Gladstone appealed to me to alter position of seats for pall-bearers; said she had asked Williamson but he was quite hopeless, I could do nothing, but spoke to W. – only too aware that unauthorised persons ought not to meddle; however, the difficulty was soon overcome, and I was put into a very good place close to Sir Henry Irving, and just in front of the Speaker.

There was an interlude of funeral music played by trombones

---

[4] The Very Revd G. G. Bradley, formerly Master of Marlborough and Master of University College, Oxford.

behind the altar screen: very ineffective, I thought. The triforiums were all full of people. Then Mrs Gladstone entered on the arm of Neville Lyttelton[5], looking very frail but gallant – an almost painful attempt to smile. She seemed a little dazed. All the Gladstones looked very worn and white, at the end of their forces.

Then a funeral march was played – Beethoven – very fine; a certain amount of wind instruments and drums in organ loft. Bridge[6] rushing about and talking – I have no doubt making jokes. Then the processions arrived. The Speaker first, preceded by heralds with white staves but in morning dress. The Speaker was quite splendid. He walked slowly and firmly, looked very impassive and dignified; an almost Egyptian face, though a high colour. Having a train carried makes anyone who is not very stately look silly. The gold-laced gown he wore was fine. The mace carried before him. One of the clerks in a wig, hollow-eyed, bushy grizzled eyebrows also impressive. Ministers first – Chamberlain [Colonial Secretary] very dapper indeed. George Curzon [Viceroy of India] looks well again. Ritchie [President of the Board of Trade] looks the wickedest of the human race – I believe he is a very good man – but he looks as if writhing under a load of disreputable guilt. They observed a sort of precedence. Old Mowbray, father of the house, whose chin had almost disappeared into his upper lip, first.

Then the House of Lords. The Lord Chancellor [the Earl of Halsbury] absolutely grotesque and made more so by the tremendous figure of Sir Wellington Talbot[7] with a silver chain and large white silk bows on his shoulders for mourning. But it is a poor thing to have a noble head, a worn and stately expression and silver hair, acquired by drawing £1500 a year from the public for fifty years and sitting in a pew like an upper footman. The Archbishop of York [William Maclagan], very pale and upright,

---

[5] General Sir Neville Lyttelton.
[6] Sir John Frederick Bridge, Organist of Westminster Abbey.
[7] Talbot was Vice-President of Wellington College and A.C.B.'s father, as first Master had found him trying and overbearing. Actually Talbot was Sergeant-at-Arms in the House of Lords for forty years, not fifty.

with a pectoral cross, walking behind the Lord Chancellor was *magnificent* – most dignified. The Bishops, especially John Sarum [John Wordsworth], who was white, elephantine and what the Scotch call *creishy*, were not great. Lichfield [the Hon. Augustus Legge] looked 25. The Duke of Devonshire looked younger and leaner and lighter than I had imagined. Lord Dufferin very splendid. There were a number of red-nosed people, like half-pay officers, who shambled in – Earls, I think. Among the barons, the leanest and shiftiest person I ever saw in threadbare clothes like a sexton. The procession closed by Vivian who was in my division, it seems a year or two ago. (I forgot to mention the sight of Sir K. Kay-Shuttleworth, pale, with tears running down his face, consumed with curiosity to see who was there, peering about, and then recollecting himself and renewing his decent grief. There were also many Eton boys – how soon the generations pass – who have been under me, even pupils like Balcarres.)

Then, I think, came the choir; some in red, some in blue cassocks, and the Children of the Chapel Royal in their pretty uniforms. As they came, they sang the Croft music. The Clergy followed. I have never seen clergy wearing orders before – two had the white crosses of St John and Jerusalem and some had Jubilee medals – and they did not look well. The two most striking figures were the Archbishop [Fredrick Temple], very haggard, pale and dusty-looking with his huge whiskers. He had no hood I think; at all events he looked all black and white – very tired and old, and so blind that he was merely led. He seemed to walk with closed eyes. The Bishop of Durham [B. F. Westcott] with leonine white hair, such a bowed little figure, deeply affected. He has lost, I imagine, his teeth as his face was all crumpled together. The Dean very small and wizened, but full of dignity. Duckworth a sort of elderly Adonis; Gore looking faded and rather dirty.[8]

The Coffin – with my father's pall, with inscriptions recording it put on, I hear, by Mrs H. Gladstone – came solemnly along, the bearers holding feebly on to it. Lord Salisbury with a skull-cap,

---

[8] Both Canons of Westminster at this time.

huge, shabby, tear-stained and a heavy brooding look, most impressive. A. Balfour languid and weary, but slim and young. The Duke of Rutland, a nobly bowed figure with dark complexion and silky white hair. The Prince of Wales, healthier and more wholesome than I have ever seen him, but with the odd look, half insolence and half timidity. He was kept waiting, I hear, just in the doorway and damned and swore at the draught. The Duke of York a poor little figure. Lord Kimberley like a respectable Nonconformist tradesman. Harcourt, large, looming and mournful. The mourners followed – all the Lytteltons; Stephen very solemn and the least worn of them all. He stood between the Prince of Wales and the Duke of York and conversed with them about something.

There were a few people in Corporation Robes and a few in uniform in the stalls. I saw Henry White and some foreigners. The Princess of Wales and a Royal party came in after Mrs Gladstone. The Princess perfectly beautiful and *so* young-looking. Duchess of York looking sulky and like a horse. Duke of Cambridge, Connaught, Prince Christian in stalls. I had seen and just spoken to Mamma as I came up, who sate just under the Princess.

The Dean came forwards and read the lesson. I was glad to sit, being faint with long-standing and agitation. The Abbey very dark (N.B. what an odd rose-window in North transept where, to get the figures of saints in, the top and bottom saints stand, the side-ones lurch and the horizontal ones *lie*, but the glass, though last century, is now well toned and venerable). The statues of the statesmen looking down on the open grave were fine, but they are too *new*-looking and spoil the effect. Lord Beaconsfield seemed to lean out and ponder – the others more impassive.

The Dean's reading was thin and clear and audible, I hear, down to the Abbot's pew, where Lucy[9] was. He told me afterwards he was much agitated and his voice nearly broke. The Rock of Ages – printed with Mrs Gladstone's translation (how my father used to dislike it) was absolutely noble. The whole abbey sang with a kind

---

[9] Miss Lucy Tait, the late Archbishop Tait's daughter.

of inward voice, a soft roar like distant thunder. Bridge may be a vulgar fellow but he accompanied that to perfection – just the right crescendoes and diminuendoes, and very feelingly. The sight of Lord Kimberley, hymn-book in air, his mouth screwed out like a trumpet, his beard working and tears trembling in his eyes, was amazing.

At the grave I could not see what proceeded. But I did not care for 'Praise to the Holiest'. The Archbishop read his prayers nobly – very loud with a strong Doric accent and sobs in his voice – but like hope triumphing over doubt. The Dean the rest. I am told that Mrs Gladstone's smile as the chief mourners kissed her hand was wonderful. Then they filed slowly out. I disentangled myself from R. Gower who wanted to talk (N.B. he was the only man who shook hands with half the House of Commons as they passed, and he looked more fantastic and commercial than ever) and walked to the grave with Mamma. It was not deep, draped with black, outlined with a ribbon of white. We looked quite a long time on the light-varnished coffin with its oak cross and the place at the foot 'Being Ascension Day'. Then I shook hands with Bishop Wilkinson [of St Andrews], who was grey with emotion.

Then with Mamma to the Deanery where we lunched quietly with the Bradleys. Poor Mrs Bradley very shaky and in conversation quite continuous, but very kind. We lunched (the Dean in cassock and ribbon) almost alone in a large shabby dining-room looking out on a quiet court. Mrs Bradley told me some interesting things of Tennyson – that if he came alone to the Deanery he wanted nothing, was easy to provide for, simple, talkative; but that it was Hallam who made the fuss. The sort of thing Hallam did was to send a message to her at 10 to 8, dinner being at 8.0., to ask if so-and-so might not be invited: he thought his father whould be interested to see him – all this not emanating from Tennyson at all. Mrs Bradley dropped compliments about me in Mamma's ear. I went to Club and read books and papers. . . .

. . . An interesting dinner at Ainger's. Sate next L. V. Harcourt who talked much of Gladstone. He said that Mrs Gladstone used to come tripping into the room when Mr G. was dying, with the intention always foremost in her mind of keeping his spirits up, and say 'You're ever so much better. Next week you will be about again and in a month quite well!' He used at last to send for Mrs Drew and say 'I cannot stand this! I want to prepare my mind for the end and cannot bear these terrible misconceptions.' He went on to say that Lady Frederick Cavendish[10] (who left Hawarden in April because it was too great a trial to her faith) treated him very harshly. Used to tell him it was all imagination, and when someone was mentioned whose name Mr G. could not catch, saying 'I don't understand', hand to ear, [she] screamed out 'Oh, don't you know Uncle William – the man who always calls you Gordon's murderer',[11] and considering whose widow she was!

He went on to say that when he went with the Brasseys to Norway with Mr and Mrs Gladstone[12], he was sitting in a chair, near Mr G. Mr G. was just recovering from sea-sickness and Mrs G., very lively, came out of her cabin, came up to Mr G. who was reading, and stroked 'the three hairs' that lay across his forehead. Mr G.'s face assumed an expression of diabolical rage, and he was just going to say something strong when he saw that Loulou was looking. The look of wrath died down, was succeeded by a flat and dull apathy which presently broke into wreathed smiles, but with rage still beaming from the corner of his eye. He said: 'I am wonderfully long suffering, Mr Harcourt!'

Loulou also said that once, when he was staying at Hawarden, Mr G. apologised for the number of *parsons*. 'I have no business to bring you into such a rookery', taking L. by the arm and leading him away.

After dinner, he said to L.V., 'We are much behind the times here: we hardly ever *smoke*. I live in a room miscalled the Temple of Peace – but there is a little room here' – leading into the little office off the hall – 'which I call the Temple of *Vice*; and here I hope

---

[10] Niece of Mrs Gladstone – Lucy Lyttelton.
[11] A reference to the unpopularity of Gladstone for his delay in relieving General Gordon at Khartoum.
[12] Sir Thomas Brassey; this was in 1885.

you will light your cigarette!' L.V. lighted one with deprecation, Mr G. saying 'If you don't take my advice, I shall have to stay till you do.'

He spoke warmly of Mrs Gladstone and her intelligence. He said that for the first time in his life, Mr G. in his illness never spoke of his state. Generally he told everything to Mrs G. – cabinet secrets and everything. Mrs G.'s sympathy was more affectionate than technical. On one occasion, Loulou had had a talk with Mrs G. about some anxious crisis and she had shown she knew everything. But at luncheon, when she was pumped, she behaved like the village idiot. Loulou had never heard such fatuous talk. He said very truly that most *women* might have kept the *secret*, but could not have resisted the temptation to show that they knew all about it. But she simply posed as a person who understood nothing, so that people often said, 'How *can* a highly strung and ambitious man get on with so hopeless a partner?'

Loulou had been suffering from bronchial haemorrhage. Sir Felix Simon, the doctor, came to see him and in Sir William Harcourt's presence said: 'No more cigarettes for a day or two.' Sir Felix had always posed as *the* smoking doctor – forty cigarettes a day. So Loulou said 'I wonder that *you* advise that!' 'Why', he said, 'I have had an obstinate nicotine cough spasmodic for years – so I have had to give it up.' Sir William said nothing at the time, but two days afterwards, came and said to Loulou 'I've given up smoking'. *He* had had a nicotine cough for years, result of 17 cigars a day. He kept this up. Loulou said 'Oh, do be reasonable – You are 70 and very strong. Don't make your home unhappy.' Sir William smiled and said: 'Oh, you're no use to me; why don't you help me in my resolution. I shall at all events try it for a few weeks – or a month . . .', and he had kept his resolution. Loulou said 'I have always admired my father, but never so much in my life.'

He said that Mrs Gladstone's calmness was due to the sudden breaking off of bromide, and told interesting stories about narcotics. The doctor who said, after talking of De Quincey to a luncheon table of men, 'I don't mind saying that there isn't one man here who wouldn't live ten years longer if he were an opium-eater. It is like keeping your faculties in the coach-house, instead of jolting them on country roads.'

He said that Mr Gladstone's spasms were horrible to see. He would talk quite cheerfully even before Bournemouth[13], about politics; and suddenly at lunch clap his hands to his face in an agony and hurry out of the room with a kind of sob.

I told the story that always moves me; that in 1889 when he dined at Lambeth, I did not have a chance of speaking to him all evening. But as I was going away, he was standing all crumpled up with arms stiffly crossed and his shirtfront in a mess near the door, listening gravely to some prating person; he suddenly disengaged himself, hurried across to me, shook my hand and said *'Floreat Etona'*.

[Volume 2, pp. 237–260]

---

[13] Between 22 February and 22 March 1898, Gladstone was at Bournemouth in the vain hope that a change of air might relieve his suffering.

II

◇

He rediscovers Cambridge; and explores the countryside round Beverley with Lionel Ford

In the summer holidays of 1901, Arthur Benson spent a few days at King's College, Cambridge. Although it was customary for Eton masters to re-unite with former colleagues and friends at the sister foundation of King's, Arthur had not himself been back to his old College for several years. His own undergraduate days had been clouded by a very deep depression from the autumn of 1882 until he left Cambridge for Eton in 1884. Subsequent failure to obtain a King's Fellowship (for which he had submitted a biography of Archbishop Laud, scathingly criticised by his former tutor, G. W. Prothero) led him to turn his back on his old College and to cancel a bequest to King's in his will. This visit in August 1901, therefore, proved very significant. Arthur met many old friends and Eton contemporaries – notably M. R. James and Walter Durnford (both subsequently Provosts of King's); he rediscovered the charms of Cambridge and of Ely; and the first thoughts of making Cambridge his future base – it was to become his home from 1904 until his death in 1925 – almost certainly came into his mind during this short stay, in spite of his lowly opinion of the Fellows of King's.

Later in the summer he spent a week at Beverley in the company of Lionel Ford, also a contemporary at King's and for many years a colleague on the Eton staff. Ford had recently become Headmaster of Repton. They explored together a part of Yorkshire relatively unfamiliar to Arthur, although his family had deep roots in the county, especially in the area round Skipton. His live of ecclesiastical antiquities is very plain from the description of the churches which he visited. On their return from Beverley, he and Lionel Ford spent an evening in London in order to attend a Henry Wood Promenade Concert. This was a complete novelty to Arthur, as was the display of 'animated photographs' in the interval.

I begin this new volume at Cambridge sitting in Monty James's big not beautiful room. His Litt.D. gown and velvet hat hang on the door – incredible dust and confusion on the shelves, and in all places where letters can be put down. It would kill me! and I am no precisian.

Sunday, August 4: a busy day. Breakfasted in Combination Room, and went to 10.30 chapel; sate next Dean as a senior master; the surplice, hood and indescribable stuffiness made me very uncomfortable; but I went through safely and with much wholesome emotion. The old stalls and windows, the organ with its gilt pipes supported by strange griffins with men's faces, all deeply impressive and lovely. I did not realise how much this place had fed my heart. But the horrible East end – a bare wall, with all the old Essex panelling torn down, now five years bare, was very painful; and the Provost [Augustus Austen Leigh], by screeching the tenor part, leaning against his stall, all doubled up, holding up music-books, was simply terrible: his mouth like the mouth of a roach. He spoils the service. They sang very sweetly and solemnly, though to my mind slow; and I don't care for Mann's playing after Lloyd's[1]. Mann creeping up a chord instead of putting it crisply down is uncomfortable. But he accompanies beautifully in an old-

---

[1] A. H. Mann, Organist and Choirmaster at King's; C. H. Lloyd, Precentor of Eton.

fashioned way, and he knows the building. Person after person went out faint. We had Dykes in F – the old morning service that I loved as a child at Well.Coll. – and two hymns.

We lunched with the Provost and Mrs Leigh, in the big dark dining-room; the garden is beautiful with its fountains and old walls; but at the end a horrible red-brick wing of Queens' looks over; and on the right is the new wing of King's – so that it has lost the sense of seclusion, but is pretty to look out on.

The conversation not interesting. Mr Leigh a sweet, dignified, simple woman – not clever or quick – but Lefroy's[2] sister!

I went to chapel in the organ-loft and sate next Mann, on the stool. The organ more manageable and improved. In old days the stops lay in steps sloping back so that the top ones were inaccessible. Dr Roberts of Magdalen was there, looking like a dissenting grocer; but I believe he is a great choirmaster. The service was beautiful and affecting, but for the Provost's cries. The windows drew me very much. A dim one of a glade (apparently) with gnarled white-timbered trees and rich figures moving. I can't interpret it, and don't much want to.

Then we went to tea in Chetwynd court, invited by undergraduates; a well-meant entertainment, but rather unsociable. I sate with Walter Durnford and Temperley, a keen historical undergrad, with a deliberate manner; talked learnedly without affection[3].

Then walked to Selwyn and saw the chapel – fine woodwork and rather a beautiful place, only wanting antiquity. Dined in hall. Phillips (O.U.B.C.) and Bromley Martin, Walter Durnford's guests. I liked P. the best: he was rather timid and asked questions of an out-drawing kind. He told me the story of Roberts at Magdalen (when the man whom he scolded for singing in the service pleaded it was the House of God). 'That's where you are wrong', he said: 'it aint the 'ouse of God at all, it's Magdalen

---

[2] Florence Emma Lefroy, eldest daughter of G. B. Austen Lefroy. Husband and wife were cousins.
[3] H. W. V. Temperley, later Master of Peterhouse.

1 Arthur Benson in 1899

2 Howden Church, near Goole, Humberside
'*I was simply stupified by the beauty of the church. The West front with fine open pinnacles, and the soaring tower . . .*' (p. 30)

3 The road between Dolgellau and Barmouth
'*We took bicycle and went down the valley to Barmouth. This was pure delight; the road was good and the tide was in.*' (p. 60)

College chapel.' This story W.D. had previously told me; as ill-
luck would have it I had hardly done laughing in my most
unaffected way, when W.D. said loudly across the table – 'I was
telling Arthur Benson the story of Dr Roberts at Magdalen today'
– and repeated it. Poor Phillips blushed silently!... Afterwards sate
in W.D.'s room and gossipped about Eton. Bromley Martin rather
a bore, I thought. Yet he is the kind of man whom gods and men
and columns agree to honour, because he is an athlete and doesn't
give himself airs. I feel in silent antagonism to such people,
probably because I am rather afraid of them and don't like being
so.

I sate next Prof Ewing who has made the fortune of the Mech.
School here; a kind plain blunt man, quiet and modest, not
exciting. We talked Alpine things. This was a crowded
unrefreshing day: and the discomfort of the morning service lasted
me some hours. Amazed at the length and breadth and height of
Newnham, representing much lavishing of wealth.

Monday, August 5: sate about, wrote letters all morning, lounged in
Comb. room; rather dim Dons came in and out. Talked about
Deceased Wife's Sisters' bill with Waldstein[4], who as usual argued
briskly and incorrectly; but he is a stimulating man. He is only five
years older than I am – and Mann is only ten. I thought them
patriarchs.

Lunched in hall: sate next [Goldsworthy Lowes] Dickinson,
rather frowsy and peaky. He beat me in Chancellor's English
Medal. But I would not change with him now.

Walked to Jesus with Walter Durnford and went to Foakes-
Jackson[5], who took us all over the College: this was full of thrills.
The tall dark Church; the beautiful ancient unvisited library – the
dignified hall with its pictures. The beauty of all this is the *possible*
union of dignity and comfort with great simplicity. The garden

---

[4] Charles Waldstein, specialist in Greek archaeology and antiquities. Changed his
name to Walsten (Sir Charles Walsten) during the 1914–18 war.
[5] The liberal theologian, who became a close friend of A.C.B.'s in later years.

very sweet, with old verbenas and hollyhocks. Saw the side of Arthur Mason's [later Master of Pembroke] dignified house.

Then to Christ's: here the pool in the garden, with the old pavilion and busts, muffled in dark leaves, was simply enchanting; so too the fellows' building – white with black stains, seen beyond the winding thickets and velvety grass of the gardens. What a treasure of recollections. Thence to John's, where we met Graves [classical tutor], red-raced and rather shambling; at first seemed deaf to me, but gradually realised me and was gracious. We spent half-an-hour in the magnificent gallery, looked at protraits. He knew none of them, got dates all wrong, remembered nothing and cared for nothing. I was struck by a feminine and ascetic picture of Selwyn, and many old fat bovine masters. But these places, for all their charm, look as if the life had somehow ebbed out of them.

Then we strolled on into Trinity, and looked at the odd and graceful piece of sculpture, without name or record, put up over the door of the staircase leading to Harry Goodhart's[6] old rooms, as his memorial. How often at one time I used to creep up there! He used to give one a quiet but warm welcome, and a bright spark of geniality and pleasure used to light up his small and sunken eye. I remember one long and curious conversation there, when he tried to pull me across the ditch into agnosticism, and the warmth with which I spoke of my religious experiences; he relinquished the subject upon that with a sort of tender pity – and I think after that our friendship rather ebbed away.

I saw too the old staircase leading up to Prince Eddy's rooms, up which I so often went. He was always good-naturedly pleased to see one, and Dalton[7] showed me much fatherly kindness. But I don't find myself weeping over the days that are no more.

Then we looked into the Bowling Green; and at the end on a bench embowered in greenness sate Hugh Macnaghten[8], rather pale and worn, in a yellow waistcoat, finger on lip reading

---

[6] Close Trinity friend, agnostic, who died young.

[7] Later Canon Dalton (of Windsor), father of the Rt. Hon. Hugh Dalton.

[8] Close friends at Eton as boys; also Eton colleagues on the staff.

Sophocles. W.D. went back to King's; Hugh took me into hall. E.W.B.'s[9] picture, copied from photographs, *rather* good, but no back to the head; but I love to have it there. Watt's Tennyson too brown and red, like a Jargonelle pear, fringed with horsehair. The boy in purple, I forget who, (Prince William of Gloucester?) as radiant as ever in the corner, and the grand Thompson.

We went and had tea in the Combination room, an ugly place, but pleasantly hung with engravings – not ancient or dignified enough, however, for such a place. Parry[4] was there, bright-eyed and friendly, sparring humorously with Macnaghten for his discontent. Macn. said that as he was going to do some higher work, he wanted *coaching*. So he went to Wyse, who couldn't take him, but recommended him to Harrison, a young man who had just taken his degree. M. went to him and hours were arranged. Meantime Harrison went and questioned Henry Jackson, who laughed and told him that Macnaghten was one of the best and most brilliant scholars of his own or any year. Accordingly when M. first went to be coached, H. received him glaring and sullen and said: 'Before we begin, I must trouble you to answer me a few questions. Have you any other motive beyond what you alleged in coming to me?' and so on for ten minutes, M. answering patiently. At last he relaxed into a smile, and said they could go on. On a later occasion they argued about *Oratio Obliqua*, and after being fosseted about a good deal by Macnaghten, Harrison suddenly slapped his book down and said 'Well, anyhow, I don't care a d—n.'

Then I slipped away and to service at King's. Beautiful chants and 'Praise his awful name', Spohr. All the surroundings for deep emotion, but I felt nothing, though the great angels blew their golden trumpets and the windows jarred and palpitated. The vergers very reverent; so that the opening of the curtain, for the procession to issue out, was full of dramatic awe; and then out came the Provost, feeling his head, and apparently trying to sidle past the verger.

---

[9] A.C.B.'s father, the Archbishop.
[10] R. St. J. Parry, later Vice-Master of Trinity.

Cambridge and Beverley

We met Arthur Sidgwick[11] in the afternoon; he seemed tired and worn. Henry Jackson with him looked rather fearful, with purple-lined eyes. He has a fatal malady upon him.[12] A.S. and H. Macnaghten came to dine at King's; so also Willert from Oxford, a genial and elegant person, with his beautiful white hair and his little imperial, like a diplomatist. He married a cousin of mine, a Crofts – so we were a very family party. I sate next A.S. and was well amused.

On Tuesday I lounged all morning, argued the war with Nixon [Dean of King's]; in the afternoon went to call on J. W. Clark [University Registrary]: found him in a bad temper with a broken arm. Mrs Clark, with her pebbly eyes, shiny complexion and large teeth, as delightful as ever. I remembered when I first saw her that I thought her appearance inconsistent with friendship; but was won by her beautiful voice and kindly smile. I liked the way she took J's hand and stroked it as we talked. J. has taken to dictating and liked it. He is an interesting person, with his great clumsy head, huge skull, a pleasant mincing lisp; a great worker, with streaks of sensuality. Now he grows old and not contentedly. His house (Scrope House) and garden very pleasant, the house like a big country-house. Mrs Dew-Smith, rather clever and pretty, came; but would talk about *Arthur Hamilton*, a subject I dislike[13].

Then went to Newnham. Found Aunt Nora[14], who slipped out to see me, like a graceful ghost or Prioress in her widow's dress, entertaining Sir R. Ball and three American Professoresses. Sir R.B. is a great clumsy man like an artisan, ill-shaved, big-boned, with a glazed eye: he had no ease or Irish rhetoric. We trailed all

---

[11] A.C.B.'s uncle, brother of Henry Sidgwick and Mary Benson. Fellow of Merton College, Oxford.

[12] If so, the malady took a long time to have effect. Henry Jackson was then 62, but his greatest honours were yet to come; the Regius Professorship of Greek in 1905 and the Vice-Mastership of Trinity in 1914. He died, at the age of 82, in 1921.

[13] A.C.B.'s first published work, a semi-autobiographical novel which he greatly regretted.

[14] Nora Sidgwick, sister of Arthur Balfour and widow of Henry Sidgwick. She was first Principal of Newnham College.

round the College, and I liked it. The great garden at the back, the cool white hall, the ranges of fresh corridors all like *The Princess*.

Then I had a nice little talk alone with Aunt Nora. She complained of shyness; told me all about her work and we had technical and professional comparisons. It was very cordial and affectionate, and did me good. She is herself like a porcelain shadow, with a pathetic eye and mouth. 'Professor Sidgwick' still painted on a door. Strolled back and dined quietly in hall. All these days the royal flag flies half-mast for the poor Empress Frederick on the University Church[15]. I wrote a few lines for the *Spectator* on the gallant, indiscreet, restless, high-principled, impatient woman; who has achieved so little with all her capacity; and has borne her hideous suffering *nobly*. I am told that she had made for herself a kind of eclectic religion, which did not stand the strain of these awful months and the shocking pain. She was anxious to live long enough to test it.

I read life of Handel – a solid, stupid man, I think; fond of wine and food, hating women and sociabilities, irascible – and utterly heavy and dreary except for an emotional sense of religion and this angelic gift. A *little* like Jenny Lind, I think, but without her tenderness. Also, a life of Mrs Ewing – rather weak – and many of the innumerable creepy stories with which the shelves are piled. I found there an old child's book of mine, given me by Mr Donne at Wellington, *The White Brunswickers* – which I carried off.

Played bridge with Walter Durnford, Waldstein and F. Whitting [Vice-Provost]. The latter plays feebly and good naturedly, Waldstein feebly and pretentiously.

Wednesday, August 7. Scribbled and read in morning; in afternoon with Hugh Macnaghten and Willert to Ely. We bicycled before a fresh wind and flew only too quick across the great flat. It was like a Constable. The great grey rolling clouds, the subdued light, the rich foliage, the long rolling lines of trees. We went by Landbeach, Milton and Stretham. I remembered a good deal of it from 1884. A

---

[15] Empress Frederick of Germany (Vicky).

farm standing in tumbled pastures, with ancient thorn trees, and the columns of an Early English church as gate-posts. At Stretham a fine church cross. As we crossed the last valley, if it can be called a valley, the country looked like Hertfordshire. I must remember the great willows whitening in the wind, and the ditch full of rich plants, teasles, comfrey, willow-herb, loosestrife and ragwort. The huge water-tower is rather impressive; the town seems to be growing. The great towers we had seen for many miles, looking grey and solemn.

We approached by the West end. The red-brick place with its wing is very stately. But the green rather ill-kept and full of squalling children. Turton, who ordained my father in 1853, was an old Regius Professor, who must have nourished artistic tastes till they turned sour. He wrote music, chants and hymns and collected *Etty's* pictures! He was old, cynical, shy and silent; and the only counsel my father received from him as he shook hands was 'Dinner at 8.0. precisely.' The Bishop himself sate at the end of the table and talked in an undertone to his chaplain, Dr Russell. E.W.B. at the Lamb Hotel; several of the other candidates played billiards on the Saturday night.

The great truncated East front with its arcading very majestic and solemn: a curious effect from the deep pointing of the stones. The porch very beautiful. We went in and strayed about; looked out to see the Prior's Door, and saw a huge lawn tennis party going on in the Dean's garden, where I stayed with the Merivales. The Deanery a huge, humpy, ancient house. Wandered vaguely and gaped. The nave splendid and the lantern extraordinarily original. I was pleased with the tombs, the rich chantries, Bishop Gunning with his dissipated Caroline face, his clothes gathered decorously about him, as though reclining on the ground. I was affected by the monuments of brave young soldiers. Macnaghten and Willert seemed to take no interest in monuments. I would not have even the most fearful taken away. This barnacle-like incrustation of human interest is what gives such a place its catholicity of charm.

The Lady Chapel a fine airy luxuriantly carved place. Then we mooned round the close; these ancient demure houses, full of old arches and windows, are very trim and romantic. The little Prior's chapel which we entered, *most* beautiful; and the great gateways. But it all seems sleepy and contented, and pompous without dignity. The sight of a large nave, unused and apparently never meant to be used, makes me wonder.

We met Bishop Macrorie[16], who fortunately did not recognise me; then round to an excellent tea at the neat Lamb, waited on by a young smart waiter, and so to the station, to find that we had looked out a Tuesday train: but there was an express in the station shunting. So we tore round and just got in and were in Cambridge in 25 minutes.

Willert very pleasant, but rather over-paced. I should like to have been alone with Hugh, who was full of intense admiration of the beauty of the place. Dined with Marcus Dimsdale[17]. A tall clean young man called Fletcher[18], whom I took to be an undergraduate and was laboriously polite to, turned out to be a leading Fellow of Trinity. The talk rather spasmodic. M.S.D. had taken a barge-full of young ladies for a trip on the Cam that afternoon. He is happier than I had thought; he is a bad lecturer and carries no weight; but he seems to like the easy sociable life of the place, in his great airy panelled rooms. But there seems a want of grip and object.

The whole place seems to me deplorably empty of men of weight, purpose and vigour. The Provost, cautious, indifferent, amiable, shrinking back the moment a thing becomes interesting. F. Whitting genial and agricultural, Brooke [Junior Dean] quite ineffective, M. R. J[ames] absorbed in antiquarian things, sociable, amusing – it all seems to me rather *feeble*, no enthusiasm. Quite content if the undergrads are *nice* – that is the word which seems to dominate everything and to be the highest praise.

---

[16] The successor to the dispossessed Colenso as Bishop of Natal. Macrorie had taken strong exception to A.C.B.'s treatment of this affair in his draft chapter on South African problems in his biography of his father.

[17] A King's contemporary of A.C.B., subsequently Fellow.

[18] Walter Morley Fletcher, Fellow and Tutor of Trinity, subsequently knighted for his services with the Medical Research Council.

Cambridge and Beverley

Monday, August 19. Got into Beverley about 8.0. and after a wrangle about a bicycle, drove to inn (Beverley Arms). Found it old-fashioned and very comfortable. A prim shy and pleasant landlady, like a governess, and a fatherly waiter. Dined just opposite the lovely perpendicular church of St Mary, ringing loud chimes; over the clean, trim, and wholesome-looking streets, the fretted towers and long grey roof of the Minster. All things clothed with the mysterious attractiveness of a new-unknown town, approached in the evening.

Slept very ill, in a comfortable room: heard the clock strike the hours round till 4.0 – though the *chimes* become silent after 11.0. Woke, however, *fresh,* and was punctual. Started at 10.40 after some fuss with bicycles and rode with speed – much too fast for comfort – over hilly country to Little Weighton – an ugly common with black trunks of sail-less windmills, a sort of recreation-ground for Beverley – up and down in dull wolds, through a pleasing village, Walkington, of pale red brick and so to Weighton station: a long wait for train. Got eau-de-Cologne out of an automatic machine for coolness. To Howden. It was impressive to see the great tower over the flat miles away. The huge snakelike curve of the Humber or the Ouse in the plain, with the Lincolnshire wolds beyond was fine. I like the great rolling lines of fields and woods to the horizon. York hung like a dim cloud of towers to the North.

Howden a clean little town of tortuous streets. I was simply stupified by the beauty of the church. The West front with fine open pinnacles, and the soaring tower with preternaturally long belfry windows, all of a grey creamy stone. Inside signs of poverty and neglect – the nave of a noble church, good 18th century heraldic windows. We strolled about: the ruined choir full of graves, the chapter-house a lovely little roofless octagon with beautiful panelled work, mouldering windows, lovely diaper. The sky like sapphire blue through every opening. All the neighbouring families seem to have annexed different parts of the building as private burying-grounds. Peered through a grate, and in a ghastly glimmer, saw the ends of Saltmarshe coffins on shelves of a vault.

Then up the tower and had an hour of purest bliss. Watched the huge view, the trains creeping through green plains, the red-tiled roofs below, etched delicately, the little streets, the old rector creeping about his garden. Then lunched at a sock-shop and started afresh.

This little place deliciously quaint but very saddening. To think of a scantily populated England building such a church, and now it falls to ruin. Partly the whole *idea* is not believed in. Schools and universities *are* believed in, and so they grow and flourish on the roots and ruins of old priories and religious houses; but the religious, sacramental priestly idea is *not* potent: we believe in mills and manufactories and trains – and so these flourish all about Howden and the great choir slips slowly into ruins. Then too how the fancy likes to dwell on the prebendaries and their Chapter-house; but I daresay they were cynical, lazy, low-minded men – much the same as the Fellows of King's now.

Sped along over the flat and turned aside to view a great grey castle – Wressle – anciently of the Earls of Northumberland. This was a huge late perpendicular pile, built of the same grey creamy exquisitely weathered stone. We got the key from a young woman in a dairy of the farm that clusters round and went to the huge ruins, with fireplaces, aumbries, stairs, chimneys all intact. The sun fell very pleasantly on the thick growth of nettles and plants that squatted on the hall floor. Elders and thorns rooted in parapets. As we came up we dislodged a pigeon which steered up out of the well of the keep into the free sky. Sate a little on the top of a dizzy tower and surveyed the view, while expresses thundered past. It stands at the end of a sea-creek, which was disgorging itself brown with mud seaweeds, all the briny oozy banks gleaming. This belongs to the Leconfields, who are Carabas's everywhere. A beautiful grove leading to the farm.

Then to Hemingbrough and found a lovely perpendicular church, still more bare and poverty-stricken than Howden – with transepts, nave, aisles and choir – old stalls of a collegiate Church, mouldering woodwork lying all about. No glass. An interesting church enough, but what does it all mean? I liked the thick tangles of some aromatic plant that grew richly all about the bases of the buttresses and even sprang in bunches in the porch. Graves slanting like stone boxes thrown down on the churchyard grass.

Outside a maundering cripple sate and talked. He had once 'followed the sea'. He had a father and sister buried in the garth. He had a little from the town, not enough; and sometimes he got a shilling or a sixpence, even a penny was welcome. He got 2d from me and the passers-by laughed, while he thanked me kindly and maundered on. Then we rode to Selby, a place hard to approach. The road will not make up its mind to go there but wanders east and north and west again. Crossed the drawbridge: it is odd to see the huge tidal creek up here so far inland, and ships building on stocks; but the abbey took my breath away. Its richness and opulence and finish, like a fine well-endowed cathedral. A grand Norman nave and a decorated choir like Howden. Here there is evidently wealth and local pride and an active rector who won't allow gratuities. The arcading of the choir very good – the whole place warm, inhabited, well-liking. But the austere ruinous melancholy grandeur of Howden is infinitely more touching. We had little time here; hurried to tea in a fussy and disturbed inn. By N.E.R. to Market Weighton, and then back in a cool fine evening over the wolds. This was all very refreshing and very impressive. I recognised all the stock-in-trade of Tennyson – 'the sheepwalk on the windy wold', 'the miles of wheat that ripple round the lonely grange'.

The wolds were once forest, then sheep-pastures with scattered trees, thorn and sloe. Then turned into farms. The farms lie couched in green banks of trees; but the view though rich, is somehow bare and wild. We wound slowly along up and down and presently began to have views of the western plains and the smoke of Hull. The Minster towers lay pink with sunset beyond the woods; and from all the wood-embowered hamlets below peered churches, towers and steeples. Thus through Bishop Burton, an idyllic village, with a porched Church and a huge pond in the centre, all lit with golden light; and then down into Beverley past the race-course, like an enchanted city.

Lionel Ford an ideal companion, talking easily, enjoying quietly, considerate, accommodating. We talked much of schools, Repton and Eton, and of people; and took pleasure in silent companionship.

Came in at the old Northgate of Beverley; and after hurried visits to the post office, dined quietly and cheerfully and wrote. I am not in the least tired by a really tiring day after a bad night – thirty miles of bicycling and a great deal of sight-seeing. The interest of the places, the beauty of everything, the perfect weather, the coolness make this day one of the happiest I have had for years. I go with Tatham[19] to the mountains, because I don't mind them, and like the result of walking and like his company – but this is the way I really like to spend my time. I gather the harvest of a quiet eye – and I have constant thrills of homely beauty everywhere. (Let me not forget the crowded church-yard of Howden, the weeping willows, the slow stream with the apple-orchard beyond, the wall of the Bp of Durham's manor, and most of all the old chapel in Fitch's house, under an umbrageous tree and the whitefronted house – also the ancient chestnuts at Wressle, and the apple orchard under the Castle walls.)

Wednesday, August 21. Today has been another extraordinary day; we went off about 11.30 by train to Hull, intending to make for Spurn Head. We drew up in a hideous station, in a hideous country; a yellowish church looking over a sooty burial ground close at hand: a black cloud drifting slowly about and taking the colour out of all things, filled the air: the smoke of Hull. This was the so-called Paragon Station. It was horribly hot as well. Then we drew out past rows of hideous houses into the country. At Hedon an immense cruciform church decided us to break all our plans. So we got out at Patrington (Patrick-town) after creeping slowly through a pastoral country – miles of wheat and rich grass-fields. Here was our first surprise: in a feeble, rustic village, with houses of

---

[19] H. F. W. Tatham, A.C.B.'s closest friend. They had been Eton boys together and were Eton colleagues. They had frequent holidays together in the Alps.

sooty mottled red brick, a gigantic decorated church that simply took my breath away. The spire curiously entwined at the base with a kind of crown of decorated arches. The place has been sympathetically restored: a new screen; chairs; the whole place looking reverently cared for. An elderly clergyman in the church pointed out an interesting Easter sepulchre. But I don't care for these antiquarian details; what I like is antiquity, combined with beauty – mellow mouldering age. The traceries very flamboyant; the whole church bearing the stamp of some *one* beautiful *mind*. It must have been all done in fifty years – and how they got the money or the labour beats me. We tore ourselves away and rushed on. The peninsula gradually narrowed. We went on a flat road, with small shrunken villages; shadowy shores and capes, lighthouses, jets of smoke from distant steamers, sea-marshes, sails dimly outlined on the horizon through the haze. We passed Welwick, then by a delightful farmhouse with a glowing flower-garden and white casements, with a sturdy perpendicular church; by a ridiculous house built by some fantastic old mariner; and then on to the last dismal promontory.

Kilnsea – a few low houses in a pastoral plain of wheat, on the edge of a huge wrinkled flat of brown mud: beyond, making a huge loop, the great sand-bar of Spurn Head which closes the Humber, like a low green island, the telegraph wire going right out to the point. At Kilnsea the road came to an end. The map says 'ruined church', but there was a hideous brick thing with white brick facings. We rode to the North Sea and there sitting on the sand ate a sandwich and watched innumerable steamers moving to and fro on a brown sea spouting smoke. The coast gradually sinks. I found a huge deposit of bones and oystershells in the brown banks. I imagine a Danish village, and the ruined church is in the sea by this time. The whole place extraordinarily bare, fresh, reviving, lonely.

Called at a little inn kept by a garrulous and cheerful old salt, who says that foreshore shooting is the way to recover health. 'A Leeds merchant came here three years ago – look at his face – why, you wanted to put him in a coffin and bury him. And now he is as well a man as you would wish to see.' There was a grey monkey in a cage in the yard that gnashed upon me with its teeth, like an old weary man.

Then we raced back before the wind – to Patrington, having been $2\frac{1}{4}$ hours away and ridden twenty miles. The good stationmaster entertained us with slow talk: told us about the vicar. Canon Morris? the 'high-learnedest' man in the kingdom. 'I don't suppose there was a high-learneder.' It is in the gift of Clare College.

Then by train to Hedon; got key at a little watchmaker's. Hedon a small neat decayed place, with a tiny town-hall and a mayor with ancient Corporation plate. But the Church!! Imagine a great high cruciform church, with traces of every style. A splendid Early English transept of the severest kind. Not over-restored, though the devilish Street[20] has got his hand in in the other transept. Again, where did they get the money and the enthusiasm? The whole is crowned by a great solid Perpendicular tower, like Merton Oxford, with many buttresses, and extra-ordinarily beautiful.

Then we sped on to Hull: a flat depressing road and slowly involved ourselves in the huge roaring town. We had no time to stop; but glimpses of shipping and docks, a tidal river covered with barges; huge fronts of flour-mills, with grumbling gear within, dusted with white – the docks themselves, a green oily pool. Got into station in good time and took train back to Beverley.

Much interesting talk with Lionel. He has a huge correspondence. He is trying to increase his official dignity at Repton without diminishing his personal accessibility. This is wise and good. He seems to me to display a laudable firmness of purpose, not to fall under local influences, to approach the whole with a sympathetic and brave spirit.

Have read *Julian Home* by Farrar[21] – what a book! – the mixture of priggishness and bad taste – the obviousness of everything said and thought. Poor Farrar! I suppose that there is no ecclesiastic

[20] George Edmund Street, architect and restorer of Churches in Victorian Gothic.
[21] F. W. Farrar, Dean of Canterbury; author – *inter alia* – of *Eric ; or Little by Little*.

more universally condemned; yet he himself forms the centre of his own picture. I have little doubt that he thinks of himself as the ascetic dean, quivering with indignation at the immoralities of the age, castigating the vices of the time by burning eloquence, moving to his place in the Cathedral with the woes of the world written on his brow, the premier Dean of England. I have no doubt that it is all rounded and gilded by the glow of imagination – yet he is worldly, insincere, hollow, egotistical to others. Still I suppose if we could not gild our own lives a little we should hardly dare to live.

That is the strength of the R.C. Church. By using confession, it makes people interested in themselves, and feeling it right to be interested; it makes everyone form a kind of romantic picture of himself or herself.

Thursday, August 22. Started about 12.0 by a road East of St Mary's, thro' a broad pleasant street into the country; had to stop for a great N.E.R. train with a green engine at level crossing. The day very hot and hazy. We hung over a bridge, and looked into a cool stream full of tall weed-streamers; at Routh, where there is a small mean church, tore [up] our plans and went to search for Meaux Abbey, once a great Cistercian house. In the wide flat, with acres of stubble – the harvest is over – we came on solid belts of trees standing up like islands, and then a great rich pasture ground, all covered with low grassy mounds, trenches full of willow-herb; an immense flight of glossy rooks rose and perched on the dead boughs of ash-trees, like the ghosts of the monks of Meaux.

I believe there is a gate-house and some grave-stones of abbots – but it was hot and we could not see them. So we merely watched the great green place with its alder-belts and ancient thorns – and horses standing in shadow. Meaux will always be to me a type of lonely placid summer, such as passes in green untroubled unvisited places all over England.

We struggled on to Waghen or Wawne; a poor church but rather a simple stately tower. Wanted to go to Swine, where there is a green mound where Sweyn, some old Norwegian, lies buried and a priory Church – but it seemed too far. The road became a lane, the lane a track, the track a green drift, in which we had to lead the bicycles; and then I felt the full charm of seclusion in that hot flat country, winking drowsily through the heat, miles from anywhere. Got to a farm called Fairholme. All along the dykes here lie the trunks of huge old forest trees, bog-oak and ash and elder, dug out in making the dyke. Then to Skirlaugh, a little dusty village. Sate in the alehouse, while a man who was graining the wall talked sententiously and absurdly about art and nature, and said things as flat as Farrar's heroes; but I was pleased that he should talk of 'graining' as a fine art, and tell a story about 'the best grainer in Yorkshire' being offended by a lady who said that she preferred the door of the opposite house to her own which he had done in his best manner, while the other was done by a mere workman. 'Give me my tools and let me go', he said. But our friend was tiresome, would not stop talking and would not imagine that we could either have or express an opinion.

Then we rode on to the little chapel of Skirlaugh – built in the purest early Perpendicular by a Bp of Durham, and chosen by Pugin to put side by side with the classical facade of St Pancras Church in an architectural book. I thought the tower too small for the church and the scheme too severe – but the details perfect.

While we looked we saw that a rustic funeral of a child had been taking place. The heavy thud of the earth falling on the little coffin came rhythmically, and the cheerful talk of the grave-diggers sounded cruel enough, while a pale-faced crying woman ran back to the little grave to have one last look . . . and the sun everywhere and the children playing in the road.

We lunched in a hedge near Rise; and the look of the woods and lodge-gate set me feeling that the one thing I have not had in my life which I should have valued is the ancestral connection and associations with *one place*. I have spent all my life in tearing up roots . . . this is ungrateful to Eton – but the work and responsibility there are always rather overclouding. I shall not begin to live it till I have left it.

Then we rode on; a strange fresh reedy smell in the air, and soon caught glimpses of the great Hornsea mere, two miles long, among its great beds of bulrushes, all speckled with waterfowl, stiff herons all round the edges brooding intently; a few skiffs sailing. Then we entered Hornsea, a dull town, with some nice old houses swamped in new streets, the Paradise of Hull tradesmen.

Went straight to the beach and lay for half-an-hour in the middle of a scene of the purest and most innocent pleasure: children digging, fathers paddling and trying to pretend they did it to amuse the children; bathing-machines lumbering down and a huge crowd watching Punchinellos and a band further down. The sea, very purple, all wrapped in haze. L.F. gave me an epigrammatic and interesting account of his masters at Repton, apparently a nice set of men but without much originality or polish: their poverty is the insoluble enigma. Then we rode quickly back. I have few distinct pictures. It was all a hazy flat with little inclines, distant woods and pleasant villages.

Last night, before I went to bed, heard a man ring furiously at the door here and the landlady remonstrate. 'He's very bad', said the man, and then followed some directions. 'I hope you'll catch him up', she said; and he ran furiously down the silent street. A doctor, no doubt. This morning a knell rang at seven, with the three triplets of tellers 'for a man'. I suppose the doctor could do nothing.

The streets are noisy here; but it is astonishing how little one cares about noise if one is not in the magisterial position of having to stop it. While we dined – our dinners increase in majesty every night – a daughter of the landlady sang operatic airs next door, heard clearly through the wooden wall. It was very pleasant: later the organ hummed in the church, very dimly lit, and we heard the voices of a chorus rise and fall.

To-night is oppressively, obsessionally hot. But I have been very happy these days, and find L.F. almost ideally congenial as a companion. Tonight we softly bemoaned the decadence of King's.

Friday, August 23. We went today to see the Minster. I am sure that the same architect that built Lincoln built the transepts. It is a most

4 An incident at Edward VII's Coronation
'*The Archbishop's homage was terrible . . . he could not rise after kneeling. He made one or two attempts and fell half over backwards and sideways. The King caught his hands and tried to pull him up.*' (p. 71)

5 The Gardens at Blickling, 1909. The upper picture was taken from the steps seen on the right in the lower.

'*After lunch, we walked out to Blickling. Since Lady Lothian's death it has been kept up elaborately – twenty gardeners – but no one admitted to the house.*' (p. 78) glorious place, and is beautifully kept. Shown round by a weary and respectful verger. I admired most the Percy tomb and chapel, tho' the former is rather *heavy*. At present the organ painted to look like linoleum, without a case, and the double open 32 ft wood like huge black boxes in the aisle is a disgrace to the building. We sate a long time on the S.W. tower and surveyed the town, with its red-tiled roofs, all the hollow interiors of streets seem to be filled with *orchards*. The town is picturesque and comfortable looking. The view was hazy. It was intolerably hot.

The absence of priests and choirs and services makes the Minster seem rather pointless – like a bell without a tongue. I felt it was rather like a beautiful stranded wreck. It is horrible to think how they swept all the rich Georgian woodwork out: there remains a fine font-cover – but a great screen and baldachino are gone. I think that the worst vandalism of all is the vandalism that sweeps ruthlessly away the beautiful and costly work of the immediately preceding generation. The *stupidity* of people who call themselves *purists* and don't see that continuity is the essence of beauty and the aroma of tradition. There is no such ting as *absolute* beauty, *absolute* taste, and if there is, no one generation can see it.

We rode out languidly to get views of Beverley. We got *one* in five minutes from the Windmill common – but the haze spoilt it. Then we rode through poor country, made dull by haze. The sky had clouded and a hot wind blew gustily. Found ourselves at Cottingham, a pleasant little town; and here was another surprise – another great cruciform church, lead-roofed. Many chattering women in the church. A fine tomb with a brass to a 14th-century rector in cope and amice, like a fur boa; rhyming hexameters all round – such false quantities! The view from the Churchyard, S.E. most splendid. This is the eighth great church I have seen in this neighbourhood.

Rode slowly back and looked at Minster again. Saw a funny quarrel between an old fat woman and a small boy, she intently accusing. He shook his hand in her face and said 'I *aint* telling a lie – and I don't care what you say!'

This is the end of a very beautiful week; full and happy. L.F.

simply delightful. But his serene enthusiasm and masterly handling of Repton makes me a little discontented. I don't want to go back to my old spade and hoe.

Monday, August 25. Left Beverley in a whirlwind of affection and respect, throwing money about in all directions. Went on 12.20 and with one stop at Grantham got to town shortly after 4.0. The day was overcast and hotter than ever. L.F. came to dine with me, and we went to the Queen's Hall Concert at 8.0.

This was a remarkable sight. These concerts of good music, played by a very good orchestra conducted by Henry Wood, are meant to prove that the British Public does want and appreciate good music. The band was really very good. Henry Wood himself is a little pale Jewish man, like Mann of King's, with black hair falling over his face. He conducts with great energy and has a delightful movement when he bends in an agony of deprecation over his desk to keep the tone down. We began with the Chopin funeral march during which we stood out of respect for the Empress Frederick. Then Weber's Oberon, Tchaikowsky, Mendelssohn (*Midsummer Night's Dream*), some Hungarian Marches (Brahms) etc. A good tenor sang solos (Hart) and a terrible young lady, Miss Goldsack, sang some Gounod sort of things. A violiniste, Mme von Storch, played well; and a fearful little man played a cornet solo. Also a stolid person (E. F. James) played a bassoon solo which provoked laughter; the high notes sound falsetto; the low notes like the musical braying of a donkey with a cough. The man himself, with his grave and dull stolidity, was half the fun. It was meant *pour rire* I think. But the best of all was an Adagio by *Waldemar Bargiel* – I have never heard of him – for a cello with orchestral accompaniment. This was real music – very soft, sweet and slow, with a structure that I could recognise.

I hate noise and speed and bangs. I think a minor Presto with drums and cymbals the most detestable noise in the world; and am more convinced than ever that the majority of people who attend concerts like merely *rhythmical noise*.

The audience was remarkable: a good many virtuosos in the

galleries; no smart people of course. There was a little grey man like Nixon, an invalid I expect, with an ecstatic poise of the head as if he was drinking in healing, a little further on. Strange long-haired men about; one rather like Sir G. Elvey, but with hair like a judge's wig. What struck me was the intense silence and attention. Smoking was allowed – a great boon.

But the pit was the remarkable sight. This was crowded by people who *stood* the whole time, in great heat, hats on, smoking and quietly listening. There wasn't the *slightest* approach to bad behaviour or even loud talk, among these 2000 people. They seemed most to be of the *clerk* type, and mostly young, though there were a few old fellows. About a fifth were women. To see all these pale intent faces listening even to the severer passages was impressive. But of course they applauded and encored the wrong things – horrible solos etc.

In the interval we went and looked at some animated photographs – Henley etc., the liquid dipping of oars into the water was wonderful; a steeplechase followed; then a very funny one of two men bathing. As soon as they were in the water, the thing was reversed so that they flew out of the pool backwards and then the clothes rushed at them from the ground one by one. The last item on the programme was a yacht, and the *King* walking up and down. I was amused at the reception of this – a sort of respectful laughter!

Yesterday (Sunday), I took tube and got into St Paul's just as the sermon was over . . .

[Volume 7, pp. 1–14 and 42–69]

III

◇

He stays at the Viceregal Lodge in Dublin, January 1902

It was by no means unheard of for an Eton housemaster to be invited to spend a few days in the holidays with the parents of boys in his House, especially if the parents were of such eminence that they could rarely visit Eton. Arthur Benson was housemaster to two of the sons of Lord Cadogan, Viceroy and Lord-Lieutenant of Ireland, and both of them (Edward and Alec) became his House Captain before they left. At the time when Arthur was invited to spend a few days at the Viceregal Lodge, Eddy had left and was at Balliol College, Oxford; Alec (later Sir Alexander Cadogan) had just been elected to 'Pop' and was to become House Captain during the year.

Arthur was reluctant to accept the invitation but found it difficult to refuse. His description of life in the Viceregal Lodge is something of a period piece, depicting the royal magnificence of the household and its protocol; the consciousness of social discrimination between the Anglican Establishment and the Roman Catholic hierarchy; and – behind it all – the sense of sitting upon a political volcano. Twenty years before, Lord Frederick Cavendish, Chief Secretary, and Mr Burke, the under-secretary, had been brutally murdered by Fenian extremists in Phoenix Park (adjoining the Viceregal Lodge). The conversation with George Wyndham, Chief Secretary, suggests a confidence in the future of the British Empire and in the expectation that 'good' could be achieved for Ireland, which was to be rudely shattered in the course of the next two decades.

Of all England I think Anglesey is nearly the most featureless – everything meanly dreary – not even looking remote and secluded; the hills too low, the houses too white, the moorland too small; not cultivated enough to be comfortable, but too much to be wild. No trees. All day a heavy gale blew, with spurts of rain. At Holyhead the waves flew high over the pier. Here I met my old pupil, Lord Kingston (formerly Kingsborough) with his handsome Countess and a little restless Kingsborough of his own. He was just what he used to be, with his dark complexion, curly hair, odd prominent nose and mouth, sweet smile. He would call me 'Sir', and raise his hat. How these impressions survive. He had been twice out to South Africa, once wounded with a spent fragment of shell, in the back of the head. He seemed very young, insouciant, affectionate; but I liked his charming ways with his little boy.

I got a little cabin and shut myself up, by lying down and shutting eyes I was perfectly well, only just faintly uncomfortable. I suppose age makes one a better sailor. A very smart carriage, with an immense buff footman, met me at Dublin, and I had worship. But I was very shy and miserable as I drove along, and wished I had never come. The sentries saluted as we drove in and again at the door.

I was handed a polite letter in the hall from Victor Corhran, secretary, to apologise for there being no one to receive me; the Viceregal party were going to the opera and were at dinner. I was to dine later with Eddie and one or two others. I was shown into a fine drawing-room and given tea. Presently Eddie came in, in hunting-costume – a broad-shirted tightwaisted coat and white breeches – looking very young and handsome. Then came in Lady

---

[1] The Hon. Edward Cadogan, formerly Arthur Benson's House Captain at Eton, then at Balliol College.

Cadogan and had coffee and talked. Last of all – His Excellency in full costume: stars, garter, and a beautiful jewelled badge suspended round his neck by a blue ribbon, the clasp a heart. This is the St Patrick's badge, and can be worn for the rest of his life by an ex-Viceroy. He wore this costume every night at dinner, except that on the quiet Sunday evening party he had no garter.

He welcomed me very cordially, said that they would have liked me to go to the Opera, but would let me off in consideration of the bad crossing; was interested to hear I had been staying with Julian Sturgis[2], who wrote the libretto of the opera (*Much Ado*). As it was by an Irish composer [C. V. Stanford], he had felt bound to go. We dined in a stately way at a little round table in a huge room – an elaborate dinner, but the mutton smoked. The dinner service with an elaborate L L [Lord-Lieutenant] intertwined. Then we withdrew and smoked. The rooms are fine but inconvenient, all opening into each other. I was told I might write and smoke in the Red Room. The pianola was played.

At last the Excellencies returned, and went into supper. I excused myself and went to bed – found a powdered, red-plushed footman fumbling with my things; was vexed at not being better waited on, but found that the Opera had rather upset plans. Found to my surprise that Clive Bigham was an A.D.C. The A.D.C.s wear a curious coat with light blue silk lining in tails and lapels, and gold buttons. They wore orders. Bigham gorgeous with a Turkish Medijic round neck and a row of little medals.

Was told chapel at 9.30, breakfast after. Meant to miss chapel but found myself in time: a shortened litany read by a long-haired delicate-handed priest. The chapel a mean and hideous room built by the Aberdeens. The house is a large low white place, stately enough, with large wings and appendages, once the country house of Dukes of Leinster. Stands in a small park; large gardens; a fine terrace in front. In the centre of the terrace a little avenue of

---

[2] Father of three boys in Arthur's House; a wealthy writer, brother of Howard Sturgis; Arthur had just returned from staying with him at his house, Wancote, on the Hog's Back.

evergreens gives you a glimpse of the Phoenix Park, so that Lord Spencer *saw* the murder[3] take place, thinking it to be a street row, from the Red Room window. There is an official look about the place as though not lived in by owners. Lord Cadogan shuts up Culford and makes it his home.

Breakfast rather awful, His Excellency not present. It was a hot muggy morning. Went off with Eddie at 10.30 in a waggonette. Drove to Christ Church Cathedral, a fine rich dim place, but externally restored past recognition. Then to the Castle – fine reception rooms and a noble hall, St Patrick's, where the banners of the order hang. The portraits interesting – some very bad: Lord Kimberley like an intellectual butler, Lord Aberdeen like an intelligent gamekeeper, Lord Londonderry like a public-house sign. Then to Trinity. We found Mahaffy[4] in a fine set of rooms, or rather a house, looking out on to a quiet garden. He was extremely friendly and amusing; but no one here seems to trust him or like him. He showed me a Czech reading-book and was horrified to hear I could hardly read German. 'Scandalous!' he said. I replied that it would be more scandalous if I had pretended to. He took us to the chapel, a hideous place with a fine screen. Showed us *splendid* chapel plate. Took us to the Library – a fine ogam stone, and gorgeous printed books: the First Folio a very poor muggy piece of printing. The book of Kells was got out for us. Odd to see such splendid art displayed in the illumination and devices, when the realism was so awfully bad – quite Japanese.

We went back to lunch; so warm a day that the inside of the library etc. was quite cold compared to open air. I had no idea that Trinity was so big or so rich. Mahaffy was very amusing all along. I told him of my discovery of the relics at Lambeth. 'I hope the Abp. gave them to the Catholics?' 'No, he put them in a case.' 'Oh, that was quite wrong; he should have given them to Manning. The Abp. would be none the poorer and Manning would have fancied himself much the richer. Now, had *I* found them here, I should

---

[3] of Lord Frederick Cavendish and the under secretary, Burke, in May 1882.
[4] Sir John Mahaffy, Provost of Trinity College, Dublin.

have run with them at once to Abp. Walsh – though I hate every bone in his body!'

After lunch the Lord-Lieutenant said that he was going to the Irish Museum. Would I accompany him? I confessed that I had no tall hat etc. 'That doesn't matter in the least – no one will mind, if *you* do not.' At 2.30 we went down to the hall, which had scarlet cloths laid down. The etiquette is for everyone to wait bare-headed while the L.L. gets in. We had a mounted escort of police, two before, two behind. I wore an agreeable black Homburg hat, while H.E. and Bigham had smart tall hats. I sate beside him and we rolled away. He was very communicative and amusing – talked about the Duke of Connaught and the indiscreet way he talked of his relations. He had said in a loud voice the other day, before a number of people 'Oh, the King is quite impossible!' I told him the story about the King telling Cromer as a special compliment, that Sr E. Cassel had a very high opinion of him. He said that the King's multiplication of orders came from his kindness and his wish to reward anyone who did him the least service.

We were received in state by Colonel Plunkett, a tiresome man with a bad obsequious manner. The Irish antiquities *most* fascinating. I had not expected anything so absorbing. The collection splendidly arranged from the earliest flint to the latest gold. The L.L. had everything brought out for me, even the great Tara brooch. It all opened up a strange dim old barbarian world. One most interesting thing was a cist with sepulchral urns complete, dug up with all the ground round it, so as to show it like a section. But the urn is upside down, without a cover and they could not explain how it was put there without the ashes falling out. It must have had a skin top which has perished.

We were guarded by police. Plunkett seemed inefficient and ill-tempered. After this I rather lost interest. We went through endless rooms, stuffed birds, agricultural produce, handed over to Professor after Professor. The L.L. had lumbago and occasionally said faintly that we must go but Plunkett said firmly that he had ever so much more to show us. At last Bigham and I developed a tendency to stand and giggle in corners, while enthusiastic savants dragged His Excellency from case to case. All the officials treated H.E. as royal, called him 'Sir' etc.

We drove away at last, a crowd having assembled; back to tea. In the house were staying Miss Corhran, very pleasant, with a soft voice; Miss Farquharson, a very serious handsome young lady, a grim Scot, who talked learnedly to me, confessed she was a prig, and lent me books. I replied that I was bound by my profession to be a prig too. I think she is a lady in waiting.

There was a huge dinner: a little Eton boy, Lord Holmpatrick, with mother and sister, a very pretty pleasant girl whom I took in to dinner; Miss Hamilton; Lord Justice Fitzgibbon, whom I sate next to, clean-shaven, interesting and amusing. Lady Cadogan had complained to me that the one disadvantage of Irish dinners was the fact that the amusing talkers all told *strings* of stories. I found Mahaffy there: while we stood and talked, there came in a tall old man, lame, with a stick, and the purple silk breast of a Roman Ecclesiastic. He had a red, rather humble and plebeian face. Mahaffy shook hands grimly, and returning to me, said 'That man ought not to be here.' 'Who is he?' I said. 'He is Monsignor Molloy, head of the Catholic University.' 'What sort of a man is he?' 'He is a beast – a low beast – and a liar as well. He ought not to be here.' I began to understand Mahaffy's unpopularity.

Suddenly the Equerry said in a loud voice 'Their Excellencies' – and they came in alone: everyone sprang to their feet, bowed etc. They shook hands with everyone, the ladies curtseying. Then Lord Cadogan led in Lady Holmpatrick, and Lady Cadogan followed with Fitzgibbon. We skirmished in after them. I was well amused with my two neighbours. The Lord Justice agreed with me about the horror of violating Egyptian sepulture.

As soon as dessert was on the table we rose and drank 'The King'. When the ladies withdrew, Lady Cadogan went out first, and curtseyed low to the Lord-Lieutenant. I incautiously bowed, not understanding the manoeuvre: each lady in turn did the same on leaving the room: went round the table and sate next Mahaffy. I asked him about Molloy. 'I will tell you', he said. 'He is a peasant and ought not to be here; he is a cad – that is what he is – he was born a cad; his education did not make him anything else, and he is a cad still.'

As we went out, the L.L. first, the Monsignor came and spoke to me. He has a pleasant humble manner; he asked questions about Eton and was very amiable. Bridge parties were formed in the inner room; and then as soon as the great people were safe, the rugs were bundled up, the pianola turned on, and there was some lively dancing. It was amusing to see Alec[5] dance with Holmpatrick, HP conscious of the honour of dancing with a boy in Pop, but Alec deserted him suddenly and I fancy that he thought I should not like it. I sate and talked to Plunkett, and grew very weary. They gradually went away. I was amused to hear that Alec had said at dinner, seeing me go and sit next Mahaffy, who splutters a good deal as he talks, with his face very close to yours, 'My tutor will want his Aquascutum.' We went and smoked in the A.D.C. room after this, and I had an interesting talk to Bigham, who has been everywhere and seen everything, about success etc. He was a loud, cheeky, not very respectable boy at Eton; very unpopular; and I hear he had to leave his regiment; but he is now in the War Office. He was a little dogmatic, but interesting. I was amused to find he thought me only 35.

I had a long talk to Lord Plunket[6], the principal secretary, son of the late Archbishop. He is a pale, fishy looking young man, with a cast in his eye, lymphatic, stout. He told me he had *hated* Harrow and thought ill of Butler[7]. He told amusing Irish stories, imitating the brogue. McGillicuddy of the Reeks seems a glorious person; huge, with a vast mass of red hair, and a screaming voice; very dishonest; going to hotels, not paying the bill, and then retiring to the seclusion of the Reeks.

Eddie went off to a ball. There was a quiet breakfast next day and I secured a peaceful morning; read papers and wrote letters. I

---

[5] The Hon. Alexander Cadogan, A.C.B.'s House Captain later in the year.
[6] Both Lord Plunket, the principal secretary, and Colonel Plunkett, Director of the Irish Museum were present at the dinner-party.
[7] Henry Montagu Butler, by this time Master of Trinity College, Cambridge.

had an interesting talk with Lord Cadogan. He showed me a horrible advertisement he had received, and asked me what I would do. He said that in his position it was impossible to go and give evidence in a police-court in such a matter. Lord Spencer had been accused of horrible debaucheries which had done much harm. I advised consulting a lawyer and he said that he would ask the Attorney-General. He asked me what system we pursued about examining boys' letters at Eton. I told him how strongly they felt on the subject. He urged that we should have some simple system. He talked a little about Ireland and the United Irish League – a political organisation. The difficulty of their position very great, between the impoverished landlords and the political agitators. But he was convinced that tranquillity, and non-interference as far as possible, was the only way. A disagreeable article had appeared in the *Times* the day before. 'They want me to resign', he said 'but I did not seek this place and was asked by Lord Spencer to stay.' He seemed in good spirits and very imperturbable. He gave me a private Cabinet memorandum drawn up by himself to read on the subject. It was a convincing document. He said that he and Wyndham[8] were perfectly in accord.

I left the Red Room for a minute; and there was a sudden bustle in the hall. Lord Cadogan went out and found the Duke of Connaught; he took him back for a conference in the Red Room; so I wandered homeless. Eddie returned; and in the afternoon we went a long stroll in the Park. The Secretary's Lodge is a much finer building than I had supposed, in a stately little park. The view was spoilt by its being dull and hazy. Eddie talked a good deal of Balliol and the tactlessness and offensive talk of the Asquiths and their following. Then to the Zoo. It is interesting that in this little hot, odorous place they breed fine lions. We saw many; I looked into a dark cage, heard a horrible growling and a puma came out of the darkness with bloodstained meat in its mouth. A nice man came round with us, but the animals received him with fury. I never saw such faces or heard such menacing sounds. He explained

[8] The Rt. Hon. Sir George Wyndham, Chief Secretary of Ireland. He was a near contemporary of A.C.B.'s at Eton.

that at this time he generally took away the bones, which they wanted to keep. We had been unable to get in by the private Vice-regal door; we asked the superintendent, who viewed us with great suspicion – but on seeing the key he became deferential, walked with us and bored us. We saw a nice monkey in a cage, with a little one. When we proffered nuts, the big one held the little one by the hair and slapped its little hands when it put them out for a nut. The bears ate minute nuts with intense enjoyment. It is odd that the animals have the *one* pleasure of eating, and yet gobble down everything so fast; have no idea of enjoying it.

I had another interesting talk with Lord Cadogan about Alec: we agreed that he wanted ambition, and *must* work harder. He thought of even removing him. He spoke very gratefully of Eton. The more I saw of Lord Cadogan the more I liked him. He seems so simple and with such an idea of duty. I think his manner almost perfect – so unembarrassed and direct and yet with much dignity. Lady Cadogan told me that His Excellency, she thought, kept the boys rather too strictly in hand – wanted Eddie to take a line of his own more. But considering the three eldest and their disasters I am not surprised. Lady Cadogan is pleasanter than I thought, more genial, and has a loud and infectious laugh which I like. It is a very happy home, though Lord C. complained that he could not see enough of the boys. He is very nice with them, asking them to tell him what they have been doing etc.

St John Brodrick [Secretary of State for War] came to dinner, and welcomed me very genially. His wife's death and his daughter's accident have given him a hard time; but he seems well and cheerful. He was betrayed into the same bow that I made, and blushed for his mistake. After dinner he sate next His Excellency and talked cabinet secrets. I heard a dim account of an anxious interview with Lord Roberts. But I had to talk to Plunket, and besides was not meant to listen. Afterwards bridge and dancing.

Sunday, breakfasted at 10. Had a dreary service at 12 in chapel, read by a dirty-looking nervous man called Hayes, who however talked to me intelligently and with great feeling about E.W.B. and the Life[9]. Lord Monteagle, whom I have met at Eton, and who is Stephen Marshall's cousin,[10] to lunch. He is a pleasant tall man, somehow like a Don. His wife much afflicted with eczema and a plump shy daughter came. Lady M. exhibited a statuette "Erin" in silver, which was meant as a present for the Chief Secretary by some ladies; by an eminent Irish sculptor – rather poor.

In the afternoon we drove to St Patrick's; the Lord-Lieutenant in state; I in a separate car, partly for reasons connected with my hat, I think, partly because I was going on to the Chief Secretary's afterwards. I was placed near the Vice-regal pew: a square enclosure under the lantern with chairs of state. Bigham sate behind them. Lady Cadogan slept in the sermon, in the sight of the multitude. By a huggermugger Irish arrangement there were chairs put sideways in front of the Vice-regal pew, so that Their Excellencies prayed into the ears of kneeling women. The Church was dark and impressive, draped in black for the Dean (Jellett) just dead. Odd spread-eagles of black on the walls. It is full of scaffolding. The old banners over the stalls are fine. 'The King of Love' as a processional. A good choir; but a temporary organ rather feeble. They sang *two* anthems: 'Whoso dwelleth' by Martin, fine and sweet; a tenor solo very good. I could not help feeling that the verging of a dumpy little man about six yards to the lectern and back was pompous and silly. The Archbishop of Dublin, a tall sad-looking man, who somehow did not succeed in being dignified, preached a stiff sermon. A dull face, I thought. The Vice-regal party went out afterwards in a hustle – badly managed. I drifted to the West door, and was fortunate enough to detect Swift's monument. *Ubi saeva indignatio cor ulterius lacerare nequit*[11] is very fine and grim. I had looked at his stall with interest, and could fancy the great face, lined and weary, with the wig.

Drove to the Chief Secretary's Lodge – a fine house. Found Lady Grosvenor, stout, amiable and vague, but very nice and

[9] A.C.B. had just completed the two-volume biography of his father.
[10] Stephen Marshall was a wealthy architect who lived at Skelwith Fold in Ambleside. He had married Annie Sidgwick, A.C.B.'s aunt.
[11] His chosen motto, composed by himself and inscribed at his request.

welcoming, dressed oddly in a low dress. Also Lytton[12], very polite and youthful, whom I was glad to see. We had a good talk. The Cadogan party there, and a stout officer, N. Chamberlain, impressively introduced to me. Lady Grosvenor told me that my letters about Hugh Grosvenor[13] had been the delight and comfort of the Duke's last days. As we were going away, she said Wyndham was too busy to come to tea but wanted to see me. We left the great bare drawing-room, with its boarded floor, which gave it an unfinished air, and went through double doors into a fine library.

Wyndham received me with real cordiality. He was smoking as he wrote; the air dim with tobacco. He sate down in an arm-chair and lit one cigarette after another. He is a fine-looking fellow, with his grey hair, bright eyes, good features; but he was hectically flushed, his hands were restless and he looked as if he was living at high pressure. We plunged into talk. He spoke of the urgent need of *men*, as the Empire grew. Of the silly athletic craze; of success – especially Parliamentary success. He believed that most people had their chance, though he himself felt that he had only taken one chance in ten. Of the number of ambitious men who found Parliament too trying and went contentedly out again. He said that the *real* pleasure was not the excitement, the credit, the success, but the *work*. He had been working all day at a dull subject – Irish Rating – but the feeling that you could *do* something for the country was the sustaining thing. He said that this was the test, whether people cared for the cheers, or for the quiet work, instancing Randolph Churchill.

He did not deny that there was pleasure in making a speech which scored, but the shadow of it was the feeling that you would have to do it again, and the sense of necessity of doing it not less well. He said that Bigham was making a mistake for an ambitious man in becoming an A.D.C. He could not study the Irish question there; it was all issuing invitation – *deeds that won the M.V.O.* His

---

[12] Victor Bulwer-Lytton (later 2nd Earl of Lytton), at that time assistant private secretary to George Wyndham.
[13] Son of the Duke of Westminster (a boy in A.C.B.'s House).

only idea of success was to multiply 'orders'. He spoke of perseverance as the one great thing in political life. The English people were so constituted that if you wore a green hat once in Piccadilly you were hooted. If you did it ten days running you became an object of interest. If you did it for ten years you became an institution to be jealously guarded. 'Dear old so-and-so in his green hat.' Most people gave up after ten days. He said that he knew I was doing my best at Eton to counteract excessive athleticism[14].

We were interrupted by a tiresome secretary once or twice, but he talked with great animation and interest, and as though he really liked to see me. Then we walked back to the Viceroy's; dined quietly, I taking in Lady Cadogan with pomp. After dinner the Lord-Lieutenant consulted me about a man for Holy Trinity. He interested me by saying that he had seen a great deal of Ingram[15], thought him charming, but had grave doubts as to whether he would *do*; whether he would succeed. Apropos of this M.B.[16] tells me that Adeline told her that Ingram would do as he liked with Lord Cadogan.

After dinner I produced my Coronation Hymn tune, and the L.L. offered to play it, which he did well[17]. His little hairy hands struck chords firmly. Afterwards he played some snatches of Verdi in a lively way – said he had not time to practise. Talked antiquities with Miss Farquharson. Bigham prattled to Lady Cadogan. Then to smoke for a little, and to bed, as I had to get up at 6.15 to catch the early boat.

[Volume 10, pp. 38–53]

---

[14] A.C.B.'s views on athleticism were to be published later that year in his book, *The Schoolmaster*.

[15] Winnington Ingram, already quite a close acquaintance of A.C.B.'s, at reading-parties with the Donaldson family at Dunskey in Scotland. He was shortly to become Bishop of London.

[16] M.B. = Mary Benson, A.C.B.'s mother, Adeline = Duchess of Bedford, a close family friend.

[17] A.C.B. sometimes set his own lyrics to music. The hymn was actually set to the music of Wagner's *Kaisermarch*.

IV

◇

He takes to the Welsh Mountains: Dolgellau

Arthur had mixed feelings about Wales and the Welsh. In 1897 he wrote in his diary: 'I don't think Wales suits me: I feel very slack and inactive there, in body not in mind, and sleep very ill.' As for the Welsh, their full absurdity was exhibited at the Eistedfodd (part of which he observed in the same year at Rhyl). They 'are like goats . . . surly, stupid and conceited. The Eistedfodd is absurd beyond the power of words', so much 'idiotic buffoonery'. Nevertheless every year from 1886 to 1899, at Easter and sometimes in the summer as well, he would take a holiday at Tan-yr-allt, near Portmadoc, the house where once the poet Shelley had lived and which Arthur's Eton colleague, A. C. Ainger, with his friend Howard Sturgis, occupied on a joint lease, using it for Eton reading-parties and gatherings of friends. 'Tan' became his base for exploration of North Wales and Snowdonia. In 1899, however, the lease expired and 'Tan' became a place of nostalgic memory, recalled time and time again in bitter-sweet moments of later years.

In April 1902 Arthur, with Herbert Tatham as his companion, decided to revisit North Wales, choosing the Golden Lion, Dolgellau, as their centre. It proved an ideal base. The holiday was certainly not inactive: they went up into the mountains, they took long walks and cycle-rides; a fair amount of reading was achieved, too, with some interesting reflections on Flaubert, Dickens and Kipling.

Welsh mountains: Dolgellau

Arthur, whose literary output was still – for a busy schoolmaster – prodigious (he had three books at press at the time), also began setting down in writing his mystical tales and ghost stories, told to boys in his House on Sunday evenings, later published under the title of the first of these tales, *The Hill of Trouble*.

For contrasting effects – scenes of natural beauty, vignettes of casual characters who catch the eye for the instant and then pass, as quickly, out of sight and mind, typically subjective literary reflections and amusing descriptions of grotesque ecclesiastical art – this passage ranks as one of the finest of the holiday chronicles in Arthur's diary.

Saturday, April 5. It rained. I went off by the 11.5, lunched at Grosvenor; repulsed a poor respectable courteous man, like a fallen butler, who went away crestfallen, shivering and deferential at the sight of the hotel porter – and then suffered stings of remorse for not having given him money. Drove to Paddington, and ran through showers and black storm-clouds to Ruabon, via Birmingham and Shrewsbury. Bought luncheon-baskets and dined after Ruabon, and so to Dolgelley. A great crowd at station and an ineffective boots. At last got off in a bus with a skittish horse: my portmanteau thrown off. To *Golden Lion* – a young and agreeable hostess – inducted into a large sitting-room on ground floor, looking into garden, and two good bedrooms. A comfortable house with nice servants.

Sunday, April 6. A fine day, sun and flying clouds. Started about 11.0. and went up hill roads, very pretty, winding about by streams; mossy woods, small oaks. One sight struck me – a pile of mossy stones, like a giant's grave, in the twilight of a larch-wood. Came out in a great valley with Cader Idris ahead. Went up a steep slope, and then got a good South view, but rather hazy. Then on to the first peak – a good deal of snow in the gullies, the rocks *rosetted* with ice to the North. Then down and to the main summit. Then past the West summit, over a huge field of grey stones and down to a road in the valley and soon dropped back into Dolgelley. The climb took about 4½ hours: met two polite men near top, who had started at nine and returned about 6.30. The great black rocky peaks, with huge rifted precipices to the North are very fine indeed. It is a noble mountain. Rather headachy and stiff, but not much tired. Read inordinately – *Bouvard and Pécuchet* by Flaubert. Found it amusing in places, boring in places – four or five quite unspeakable episodes. The view of moralities is totally different. Dined well.

Monday, April 7. Shopped and found a circulating library. Then bicycled all *round* Cader Idris. Up to Cross Foxes, walking most of the way. Then to the head of a pass under Cader. Fine rifted rocks, overhanging road. Then by an embanked road, a good run to Tal-y-llyn, a large lake. This great wide bare valley, with huge hills all round, and wild glens going up secretly into the hills, very grand. I could stay at one of these inns with pleasure. Then a long run down – a huge low oakwood, very red, with Preraphaelite firs to right; a toy railway, a merry old man in a truck running down who waved his hand to us. Then by a village, and finally out into the wide Towyn valley, the hills on either side sloping to sea. Passed a nice country-house with good trees, near Towyn, but had to hurry. Caught train and on to Llwyn-gwril, a small village, with horrible new houses; then by road to Arthog. Fine views of Barmouth, blue sea, red sands, green estuary. Arthog a nice place. Tatham knew it well. Beautiful houses all along here, on the high wooded hillside. Then in about 4.0. Shopped; got shoes altered; wrote letters; read *My Trivial Life and Misfortune*, a book Uncle Henry[1] liked, very pathetic and humorous; and then wrote diary. A good day, passed without fatigue in some of the most beautiful scenery in England[2]. The cold bracing wind is very pleasant. We have our

---

[1] Henry Sidgwick.

[2] A.C.B. persists in referring to Wales as 'England'. He does so in the earlier passage on his visit to the Cadogans in Dublin, describing Anglesey as in England.

meals in the sitting-room, and so are not troubled; we have plenty of books. These days are like a pleasant medicine. They make me hungry, sleepy, contented – not originative and not receptive. I find that I tend to read rather than to write, and the hours pass very quickly and pleasantly.

Wednesday, April 9. Yesterday we took the 10.30 and went up the valley to Llanuwchllyn. Here I bought a strong stick with a stagshorn handle. Then we set off slowly up the ridge of Aran. We passed a hill with a ragged staff on it; saw snipe, curlew, hares. We reached the top of Aran Benllyn in under two hours. I was sickish and uncomfortable the last half-hour; it was steep and not a breath of wind. Lunched here, which made me all right for the rest of the day. Picked up a small india-rubber cup. The view into the corrie behind Aran is very fine indeed. The side very steep and craggy; at the bottom a cold stream runs through great green fields, and a huge green smooth mountain rises opposite – an extraordinarily desolate place – green and brown. Great smooth hills everywhere in a haze.

Then along the ridge to the true top – Aran Fawddwy, with a big cairn. We had plenty of time at our disposal, so went on and peeped down another green dale, going to Dinas, with a crag opposite. Then slowly down to Drws-y-nant station. Saw a few grouse. Talked for some time with the stationmaster in the signal box and endeavoured to learn the staff system of block-lines. The intelligent explanations confused me. Saw the odd leather pads on which they hang the staff at night or when the train doesn't stop. Got back about 5.0. and had tea. Wrote a good deal of a story in the evening, the *Hill of Trouble*. We talk out plots as we walk and Tatham is very inventive.

Today, Wednesday, is one of the best expeditions I ever recollect. Cold and fine; we took bicycles and went to the Cross Foxes, then took the left turn, by bare hillsides and over a col to Dinas Mawddwy. The view after passing the col, most splendid: huge green smooth hills rising very steeply, a stream running at the bottom. The valley curves greatly, and mysterious green valleys run up into the heart of the moorland. A huge hill by Dinas has been planted with larches, which made steep lanes up to heaven, with the sun shining down the green glades. Swiss. A good house, with a concrete wall on left. Got gingerbeer at Dinas, and found that the house was a Dipsomaniac retreat of Dr Walker's. The idea of these tragic persons shut up in this beautiful lonely valley for six months or a year for such a purpose cast quite a gloom over me. What do they do there? Think of meeting people, under the same conditions, at meals day after day.

Then on towards the Bwlch-y-Groos – a long, winding valley, with two or three nice houses – the same huge smooth hills. Then we lunched by the road, opposite a craggy col where the water fell steeply down and roared like an express train. Here I had an altercation with a farmer. Owen Jones, who threw huge stones into the road while sowing and narrowly missed me. 'I know I ought not to have done it', He said plaintively in answer to my imprecations. Then we pushed the bicycles up a very steep hill-road, opposite a huge scarred hillside of ragged rock – a sharp arete over us. This was heavy work. We reached the top at last, among grassy hills. It is 1795 feet high and must be one of the steepest carriage roads in England. Then we descended gingerly a steep and stony road; my brakes very useful; and came down the long open valley to Llanuwchllyn. Here the marshy looking road to Lake Vyrnwy, the new huge reservoir, with a submerged church, turned off. We might have caught a train, but we scorned it, and had a delightful run to Dolegelley of twelve miles, after a little climb to the col. Got in about 5.30. This was a beautiful run and a fine ending to a splendid day.

Thursday, April 10. I sate and wrote letters half the morning – 24 or so. In the afternoon we walked up by a place called the Torrent walk, where a stream comes down in a wood, among mossy stones. Very pretty but not entrancing. We lunched at the top of the walk; then by a Quaker's burial-ground and rather an original new church to Bont Newydd station, and then up to Nannau through woods, by an odd deserted house in a grown-up garden.

Welsh mountains: Dolgellau

A locked gate, and an impregnable lodge, but the keys were hanging up. So we went like magic knights through the high deer-park. The house plain and ugly. Then by a lake and round the precipice walls – a very pleasing place. The path is dug out of the face of a very steep heathery *brae*, and has fine views. Then by a mysterious tangle of roads backwards and forwards, by some pleasant farms and in by 6.0. We had been about 15 miles, I suppose.

Friday, April 11. Took train, changed at Bala, and were entertained by a drunken man who took me for *Mr Mostyn of Mold* and begged pardon for speaking his mind. My face is of the vague Teutonic type that looks like everybody else, and I am not infrequently taken for someone else. Then to the Arenig station, a place in a fearfully desolate moorland. We started thence about 12.0 and got to the top of the Arenig (2800) in a hour, going fast: a fine but hazy view. Lunched on the next peak. My orange ran down hill hotly pursued by me. Then slowly down by grouse-butts, moorlands and farms to Llanuwchllyn. Waited for train in a room hung with bacon; a polite landlord. Back about 5.0. I am not getting on with my work, and have read only eight books of Homer. A bad wakeful night.

Read *Emma Bovary* – in a translation. I suppose the style must be good. The descriptions are very fine and minute; but I don't think the whole thing artistic. I don't think it *typical*. Not one in a million women would abandon themselves as she did and then kill themselves at the end. It does not convince me of truth; and the study of detail obtrudes itself. *Bouvard and Pécuchet* is simply ludicrous. These men could not have flown from one subject to another. If they had stuck to one and made asses of themselves in it, it would have been likelike. But there is no more verisimilitude in two copying-clerks taking up fifty subjects in turn with this wild enthusiasm, than if they had had fifty diseases in turn. A good parody of the book could be written on these lines. On the first day of the convalescence from smallpox, diphtheria sets in; on the first day of convalescence from this, pemphigus. This would be just as true to life. Not physically *impossible*, but about as likely as the other. You can't see the wood for the trees in these books; and the want of *subordination* of which du Camp and Bouillhot accused Flaubert, in the case of St Anthony, is true of all these books. *A book should be a picture and not an album of photographs* – so thinks the great Twalmley.

I am much disappointed in the *Iliad*. The men are feeble; the gods *fatuous*. Their interference spoils the *whole* story, and it is incredible to me that the listeners should not have felt this. But it is impossible that the Odyssey should be the work of the same hand or hands.

Read some of Rudyard Kipling's *Day's Work*; thought it most feeble. Also Forster's life of Dickens, which makes you feel as if Forster was dodging about and trying to get in front of Dickens whenever you wanted to look at him. Dickens was an *actor* by nature, a sentimentalist and I think a cad. Hs is very humorous and his melodrama is good; but he had no inner dignity.

Saturday, April 12. We took bicycle and went down the valley to Barmouth. This was pure delight; the road was good and the tide was in, Cader lay like a great black bastion over the hills to the left. At Barmouth we were undecided, but eventually rode on to Llanbedr – a dull road, small and starved green fields surrounded by grey stone walls; a mean landscape, not pastoral enough to be comfortable, not wild enough to be impressive. Lunched in a little lane, among violets. Then on to Llanbedr and a little way up the pretty valley. I rather want to see Cors-y-gedol, a house with a fine gateway, but the road to it looked depressing: a long steep sort of avenue. Here were huge heath-fires, throwing up great columns of smoke. It was along this road that Tatham and I walked in 1888 on our first visit to Tan. We had bicycled to Aberystwyth from Eton; and having a long time to wait at Barmouth, decided to walk. I remember I was very footsore.

On the way back, annoyed by a cyclist, with a peering face, like Nixon [Dean of King's], whom we overtook, and who then rode about three yards behind us to Barmouth. This irritated me inexpressibly. When we got near Barmouth he tried to pass us, but I could not stand this and raced him and won in great style. Tatham laughed insolently. We crossed the viaduct, having to wheel our cycles through soft sand, and to Arthog. Here we explored the fine old hotel, a sort of castellated house built, I should say, about 1800, where Tatham was in 1874. A nice garden and well placed; looking out to the estuary among innumerable wooded mounds of rock. Then to the Falls, and so home. This was a delightful ride; fine but hazy weather, very cool, about 35 miles.

Tatham reminded me of a boy giving in a paper an answer to the question as to what Charles I's last words on the scaffold were. He replied: 'Don't let poor Juxon starve', muddling it up with what Charles II said about Nell Gwynn. It suggests an old fox-terrier!

Sunday, April 13. Finished *Schoolmaster* proofs and sent them off to Murray. Started about 12, a strong SW wind blowing; walked to Gwanan lake, and then took a footpath towards Cader. We got to the lake under the summit and up the Fox's Path – very steep and loose stones. At the top of the shoulder I declined to go to the main top; thinking it a long way off; but afterwards repented. It took Tatham two hours ten minutes from hotel to the top. The view was glorious: Criccieth Castle, Bardsey Island, Snowdon – then Breidden hills, near Shrewsbury and the Wrekin; we could see Plynlimmon very clearly, and the Pembrokeshire hills and the South promontory of the Cardigan bay. Practically a view of the greater part of Wales.

We stole back along the ridge the way we ascended it last Sunday, through pleasant little Alps and steep paths, by falling streams and came out just behind the town. In at 4.35.

Monday, April 14. Started about 11.0 and bicycled to Trawsfynydd. We tried to find Cymmer Abbey (or Vanner) which lies on a green promontory over the Mawddachs, but we got up above it, and all we saw was an arcaded wall among apple-trees. Then along a fine valley, with woods and high heather-clad hills. Many good houses; then the two Rhinogs and Llethr began to appear on the left, rising over the woods, and the embattled front of what we used to call Diphwys from Tan. We crossed a desolate moorland by a straight road – evidently Roman – stopped for gingerbeer at an inn in Trawsfynydd, over-smartly furnished but with an old spinning-wheel. Then on to Maentwrog. On the right we saw a high green tumulus, Tomen-y-mur,. about which Booker [Eton colleague] had told us. I see from the old map that this is close to the old Roman road. Then we left our bicycles at a little house in Utica and walked to the tumulus. About 150 yards due West, or WNW, in a line between the top and Moel ddu is the obvious foundation of a square fort. But the place is wonderfully chosen. You can see Cader (South), the Arenigs (East – only *just*, from the base of the mound they are not visible); Snowdon, just visible, over Moelwyn, and to the West, the sea by Portmadoc. I don't suppose there is a place in N. Wales that gives such a *conspectus* of mountains. I wondered what old chief lay beneath. I think it must be British rather than Roman. Then we went down again. It was pleasant to make out all the *Tan* landmarks. We thought we could see the house, under the cliff. We could see exactly where it was. Tan-y-bwlch was quite large, and the road from the Tan-y-bwlch station that we have crossed many a time in the old Tan days. I can't feel it is all gone; I feel as if it would be all the same there if I walked in.

I must add that this morning we saw the Church, and were seized with hysterics at one window – the Crucifixion. The Virgin, in pink, is extended on the ground; but the scale is all wrong, and a woman on her knees who looks rudely into the Virgin's face is so big that the Virgin looks like a doll. A figure behind, with a face like Walter Durnford, creeps up as if to bite her. Behind the cross rides a man with a spear, which he manages to thrust into the foreground, though he is about a hundred yards away. Moreover his horse disappears into the Cross and never emerges.

This is a great transparency. But I would not take it down; it is better than Mr Kempe's[3] windows; of course it is grotesque, but I

---

[3] Mr C. E. Kempe, ecclesiastical artist and designer who lived at Old Place, Lindfield, near the Benson home at Tremans. Arthur derived constant amusement from his windows.

don't mind that. They have good stalls, pulpit and episcopal chairs. The Church is roofed and pillared with wood.

We go back tomorrow. We have had a wonderful time here – perfect weather and absolute success in all our arrangements. I find I have a love for this little grey, close-built town and for the pleasant friendly people here. Certainly if one lived in Wales, this neighbourhood would be delightful; but one must not forget the summer languors, from which we have been saved by this beautiful cold fresh wind. The privet hedge is green in the garden here, and the trees all sprinkled with buds. A great sprawling shrub under the windows has come out since we have been here in big yellow flowers. I am very grateful for these days of happiness, which might almost have been planned for us to be delightful – I have little doubt they have.

Tuesday, April 15. The holidays melt away. We left Dolgelley by the 10.35. Showered tips in all directions, and expressed unalterable regard. The landlord is a scented young gentleman, I should think really a gentleman, who is kind to us, *very* nice to his wife and children, has a farm and hunters, and 25,000 acres of shooting. He wears top-boots and is a great swell; a little pinchbeck perhaps.

We found a coupe, and sate in it at the end of the train – a very new and pleasant sensation having the great views clear behind us. The rapid running of the track as we flew along, very odd and bewildering. We managed to get the guard to keep us the coupe, so we travelled in huge comfort and state up to town, with a yellow ticket on the window to say RETAINED. It rained heavily. It has kept fine *exactly* for our visit. I got immersed in a Wilkie Collins, and was oblivious of all else.

[Volume 12, pp.44–63]

V

He attends the Coronation
of King Edward VII

The coronation of Edward VII was due to take place on 26 June 1902. About ten days before, the King was taken ill, appendicitis was diagnosed and peritonitis rapidly set in. The King was determined to go through with the ceremony at all costs, and the will of his doctors did not prevail until the morning of 24 June, while the dress rehearsal for the ceremony was on the point of beginning. To everybody's amazement the King recovered sufficiently for the coronation to take place on 9 August.

Arthur made his own contribution to the service by supplying appropriate words to the *Kaisermarch* of Wagner, which was played at the conclusion of the service as the King and Queen moved in procession out of the Abbey. Very naturally Arthur was present; and very characteristically his roving and disrespectful eye picked out the elements of the grotesque, the absurd, the ridiculous and, of course, the sublime. One wonders if a fuller account of this splendid occasion has ever been recorded. As with all great ceremonial occasions, much of the fun and excitement took place in the moments of anticipation before the service and in the sensation of relaxation afterwards. This account begins, then, with Arthur setting off by train on the day before the event (and cheerfully putting an Eton boy at ease on the journey by inviting him to smoke), meeting his old friend and former tutor from Cambridge days, Bishop J. E. C.

Welldon, Canon of Westminster (only recently returned from the bishopric of Calcutta). It ends with the street scenes after the King and Queen have moved off to Buckingham Palace, with street urchins taking advantage of a quiet corner off the royal route to play a game of make-shift cricket.

This is the longest single episode described in the diary The entry for 9 August 1902 covers thirty-three diary pages.

Met Trant[1] at the station. There is something in what Mrs Bramston said. He is deplorably unbraced. He was in grey trousers and a black tie tied into a Roddy Owen collar that looked like a dilapidated park-paling – it was so wide and tottery. In our carriage (the train very crowded) was young Bovill (at Vaughan's); opposite me sate a man I know, who knew me, but we were happy each in thinking the one did not recognise the other (Elwes?). Bovill had fled from me on the platform, shaking hands, and had rushed (evidently) for a secluded smoking-carriage to smoke unseen. After a little while I said to B. 'Don't you smoke? I hope you won't abstain from smoking because of me.' He laughed and blushed; said his mother didn't mind it, and presently smoked. His good humour, at our appearance in his chosen haunt, was great – and proved him a gentleman.

Martin [Eton Servant] met me at Waterloo and took my bicycle off to Victoria. I to Barton Street[2] where I found M.B. and Lucy. It is a very pretty and homelike place, with its little panelled rooms and nice china, but it is rather pervious to sound and smell and is not quite on my scale. I have to walk gingerly.

Walked out and met Vice-Provost [F. Warre Cornish] in Dean's Yard. He was lodging in Cowley St. We met the Bishop of Oxford [Francis Paget] walking and had a short talk. He was amused to find himself supporting the Queen – and pleased –

---

[1] Trant Bramston, assistant-master at Winchester. A.C.B. met the Bramstons while staying in the temporary family home at Winchester (St Thomas' St).
[2] Lucy Tait's recently acquired flat, near the Abbey.

thought it was because of his father, not local[3]. He was full of emotion about the King and the illness – the stoppings of his teeth more visible than ever, as he smiled elastically. But he's a dear! While we stood there, an escort of horse guards clattered up with a coach, with redcoated coachman and footmen. The Dean [G. G. Bradley] (who looked very small and frail and who has just resigned, I hear) and Canons came out. It was the Regalia arriving. They were brought out one by one in such ugly modern cases – red velvet and black leather – crowns and sceptres. Looked up and saw Herbert Ryle (Exon) waving on a roof above. Took V.P. back to tea and went out again with Lucy to try and get music. There are but few decorations and few signs of pageant. There are big light-green doors with huge gate-posts of wood across a few streets, ready to be locked at dawn tomorrow. We were referred from one place to another – a civil Inspector at House of Lords. At last we went to Welldon. Found him very excitable and full of talk of a loud melancholy kind. 'It is hard, my dear Arthur, to sit in these beautiful rooms – which I would point out to you have generally been tenanted by Harrovians[4]' (here he looked round with a pathetic smile, gave a convulsive quiver and struck himself on the chest) 'and to reflect that I am an ABUSE – an Abuse, I repeat.' But he said many interesting sententious things as he rattled on. 'Do as you like, my dear Arthur – say what you like, do what you like – to be straightforward is the privilege of friendship. Not that you would ever be otherwise – it is characteristic. The Dean said to me that some of the choir ought to be heavily sate upon, when I was in residence, for misbehaving. "You must do it", he said. "You may be sure", I said, "that if I have any sitting to do, I shall do it heavily"' – so he flowed on.

He took me to see his study. I commented on the beautiful court. 'Yes', he said. 'That house opposite is the Earl of Portsmouth's – a soothing thought – but, my dear Arthur, one who has once looked out upon the heathen cares little to sit and look out on that court.'

---

[3] His father was Sir James Paget, surgeon to Queen Victoria.

[4] Welldon had been Headmaster of Harrow before becoming Bishop of Calcutta.

He said to Lucy, 'the house is more respectable now than it was.
When it was a monastery all the rooms were full of tobacco-
smoke. This was when Gore used it for the Community[5].' It *is* a
most stately and beautiful house, badly furnished (tho' expens-
ively) and the approach, through the dark smoky cloister, with the
mouldering stone, then a white tunnel, then a little smoky barred
court, with a sooty fig tree (the house lies back through a sort of
little garden) – [is] a little vulgar.

He took us off in search of Bridge[6], whom we met with a lady.
Bridge was all kindness and vociferated loudly and freely,
hobbling on, full of excited talk. We went to his house which was
all in confusion as he was packing to go off to Scotland – a gloomy
panelled, nondescript place. He took me to his study and gave me
an Alto Copy[7], used in the Abbey; introduced me to his son, a
Charterhouse master; wrote an inscription in the copy; chattered
away about salmon – spluttering, but inexhaustibly kind. At last
we got away. Lucy was gravely shocked, thinking Bridge was
drunk! But it was only his usual vein.

We dined very quietly and went to bed early. Of course I could
not sleep; and at four was awoken by a peal of ordnance (at the
Tower?). The house was astir early, and we assembled, a funny
party, at breakfast – Lucy and M.B. in full court dress with feathers
and lappet and I in velvet, with steel buttons. We breakfasted.
Winton[8] came in, rather in a fuss. But he said that never was a King
in a better position for making a fresh start. He had been given just
the things he wanted – romance, suffering, interest – and he had
gone to the operation with such splendid pluck, thinking nothing
of himself. He said 'I wrote this to him – all of it – and practically'
(this was a characteristic word) 'asked him to make a new start. He

---

[5] The Community of the Resurrection. Gore had just left Westminster (where he
had been a Canon) to become Bishop of Worcester.
[6] Sir John Frederick Bridge, Organist of Westminster Abbey.
[7] This was a copy of the music of the *Kaisermarch*, which he and Lucy had gone in
search of earlier.
[8] Randall Davidson, soon to become Temple's successor as Archbishop of
Canterbury.

received it most gratefully and said that he appreciated my motives and quite understood the position, and that he was genuinely and sincerely anxious to do all that he could for the welfare and wellbeing of his subjects.'

He went on to tell me that the King had given him the insignia of the K.C.V.O. – star and badge – thought he had earned it, but said he could not knight him. I said 'What about Edie?'[9] 'Oh, she doesn't at all want to be "Lady"', he said, 'that won't be necessary'. I said I thought it would be a *great* pity if she was; it would give great offence among ecclesiastics etc. He looked a little troubled and said something about precedence. He went on to say that the King was going to give the Archbishop an Order – a gold cross on a gold chain, not to be worn except by Royalties. I really think the King is mad about Orders. I hope he won't make himself ridiculous. That they should be very sparing and very real is the *only* way to make them worth anything whatever; and I am rather ashamed of the English people for thinking anything of them at all. Edie came to the house to dress; and finally we all set off about a quarter to nine. I found myself serene and interested – what nonsense it is to let things seem difficult or arduous beforehand – one must take them as they come. The street, owing to the barriers, was very quiet – nearly deserted; a strong force of police. We soon got to the Cloister door. The cloisters were full of ambulance tents with beds and armchairs for fainting or epileptic persons. We were gradually separated. I went up steep stairs, and eventually came out of a vomitorium near the aisle roof. I was shown by an obliging officer with a red baton, to my place – Hodgson of Austen Leigh's[10] – at Eton with me. My place was the last on the top row, assigned purposely to my insignificane; but it had this enormous advantage – that by leaning forwards I could see right into the choir; and though I could not see the thrones owing to pillars, I could see the peeresses' seats and the steps of the footpace. The place filled slowly. It is quite impossible to describe the scene at all. The

9 Edie Davidson was Lucy Tait's sister (seventh and sixth daughters of Archbishop Tait respectively).
10 Edward Compton Austen Leigh, Lower Master of Eton.

galleries were very steep, so that we could all see down into the nave. Opposite me in the galleries sate mostly girls and young women. In front rows, children – minor sons of peers – nice little boys in court suits. I noticed Clifton and Roos. One little boy played so much with his gold-hilted sword that his mother took it away. Our side was mainly men – diplomats all round me: Headlam, in a magnificent coat (he told me afterwards that it was borrowed and of much too high a grade) and next me a smart young Foreign Office man. I talked to him and he said he was a Westminster boy in 87. He began to talk about the Archbishop and his cope. I said: 'My father' – it is always better to do this, I think, in case people say awkward things. He looked at me, and then said 'Well – and how's Hugh, then? I was up at Trinity with him.'[11] I disencumbered myself of cocked hat, tickets and sword by putting them into a curve of the vaulting close by me.

Down below the costumes were very magnificent: the Knights of Orders in full robes. The red of the Bath is fine, but the Michael and George – a dark blue – even finer. There were abundance of gorgeous uniforms and academic silks. Some judges came in, and I think that a judge *moving about* looks ridiculous – like a bogy. After a bit a procession came in of men in odd copelike robes, barred with gold who stood by the choir door. These were Cinque Port Barons. It was too dark for me to recognise much. The peers and peeresses kept arriving, looking very splendid in sweeping robes, and I could see them taking their places beyond. The centre space was carpeted with rich blue, and lights burning low. The time moved slowly on – the procession of choir etc. went down to the West. Then princesses with long trains began to arrive. People stood or sate and there was loud talking. I read my book philosophically, talked or looked about and the time was not long. The sight of long-trained flashing persons sweeping up the choir steps like peacocks was very beautiful. In fact it was all so rich that it looked theatrical, as if it could not be true.

---

[11] A.C.B.'s youngest brother, Hugh. Later, Monsignor R. H. Benson; in 1902 he was a member of the Community of the Resurrection at Mirfield.

Then the Prince and Princess of Wales arrived, he looked perky and common. Then the *Queen* – most beautiful, leaning on the Bishop of Oxford's hand, he oddly bowed over it, in a stiff cope.

The choir were on both sides just to my right. I saw Lloyd [Precentor of Eton], and several eminent musicians in Doctor's Hoods. Someone – Parratt?[12] beat time in the screen centre, which was followed by a conductor on each side, so that the music was perfect; but I heard so much of the tenors where I was, that it was not very balanced. It is of no use recounting the service. The arrival of the King was the great excitement. It was preceded by a long pause – the clergy had passed – the Archbishop walking more strongly than I had hoped.

Everyone was very nervous about the Dean. He was quite dotty. He was for ever saying in a pause – 'Might not I do this? I think I might do this?' whether there was anything to do or not. He feels acutely being allowed hardly to do anything. The Archbishop is very weak on his legs, very absent in mind, and so blind that the service has all been specially printed for him in huge black letters.

The pages looked very delightful, especially when they sate, a row of elegant red figures, on the edge of the footpace. A. Balfour looked very slim and graceful. The peers carrying spurs and swords were not grotesque – yes, I think Lord Grey de Ruthyn holding a spur as if it were a curious beetle was. The Duke of Grafton with 'Curtana', the blunt sword of justice, was fine. Lord Roberts was too much under me to make out. There was a delightful little page of about 8, carrying a huge coronet and enjoying himself thoroughly, though he had to take a run, after looking carefully round his burden, to get up the choir steps. The King himself with an odd red cap on, walked easily enough, though slow, and looked majestic – rather gray.

The service I could hardly hear at all – except odd provincial and guttural vowels from the Archbishop – here and there a word – and the King was inaudible to me, except as a kind of hoarse grunting.

---

[12] Sir Walter Parratt, Organist at St George's, Windsor.

Coronation of King Edward VII

The Bishop of Ely [Lord Alwyne Frederick Compton] sounded like a faint echo. I heard Winton's Gospel. The putting-on by the peeresses was a funny sight and I am bound to say looked rather absurd and very shoddy. M.B. says that it was succeeded by a lightning flash – they all looked at the little mirrors in their fans to see if they were straight.

When the peers put on their coronets, the Cinque Port Barons put on curious black velvet caps. The actual ceremonies I could not see – behind a pillar – but I could see everyone coming and going and a glimpse of the King's crown over the back of the chair.

The scene of the homage was fine, though the group of peers waiting, one of them trying to support his tottering frame with a slender wand, which collapsed each time, was funny.

The Archbishop's homage was terrible. He had already made a fearful series of mistakes in the prayers: instead of telling the King to support widows, he said 'widowers' and so forth. He made long pauses and everyone was very anxious about him. When he went to do homage, the Bishop of Winchester said, he could not rise after kneeling. He made one or two attempts and fell half over backwards and sideways. The King caught his hands and tried to pull him up. Several people said that they thought he was kissing the Archbishop's hand (I believe he *did* kiss the Abp.'s hand). Then he said hurriedly to the bishops near him 'You had better help him, I think.' So they closed in and got him up, but his legs gave way under him like a doll's legs, and they had to carry him by main force to his chair. The Bishop of Winchester went and said 'Can I get you anything? There is some sal volatile close at hand.' To which, in a loud voice, the Archbishop said 'No! I don't want anything at all. Go away – I'm all right' – and so he was. He said afterwards at tea that he was not faint, but simply his legs failed him; age had attacked him there. He added 'I had made up my mind to get up on my *right* leg, and they pulled me over on to my left leg. It was kindly meant, but upset me.'

Further disasters were in store. The moment the ceremony was over and the King withdrew into his Robing-room to divest himself of some of the masses of drapery, the Archbishop was

71

asked, at his command, to come in to the ante-room and rest. 'I went in', said the Archbishop, 'and took the only chair in the room. In a moment I smelt the steam of broth. The King had sent me a cup of soup, which I drank. Then he came in himself to ask me how I felt, and in getting out of the chair I nearly fell down – and I could not stand.'

But the worst of all was in the Communion. He could not see where the King was, and went to quite the wrong place to administer and nearly put the bread on the carpet. He was guided right. The King looked frightfully nervous at the Archbishop's movements.

The service slowly proceeded. The flare up of the light when the King was crowned was very fine, but it made it feel more theatrical than ever. Then came the processions away. As before, the Queen looked lovely and the crown suited, not so the King. The crown looked too big and heavy. He looked like one of the Kings in *Through the Looking-Glass*. My own little contribution, the words to the Kaiser-march, was spoilt because the Choir were so anxious to see the King depart that they did not attend or sing, and the result was awfully feeble.

As soon as it was over and people began to slip away and the storm of cheers outside was dying down – by the way, the cheering in the Abbey was very spontaneous but felt irreverent – I went with Headlam right along the galleries and looked down into the area. It was now exactly like the garden-party in *Alice in Wonderland* – the business-like peers had gone, but the rest evidently yielded to the irresistible desire to prance and pace and mince and look magnificent, reading admiration in each other's eyes. The coronets were truly absurd – so big, like battered red hats and so *unreal* looking. The peers who took them off looked well. I saw Cobham below, sitting in melancholy seclusion, and many people I knew like Aberdeen, Mostyn etc. etc. After a little, while we watched the judges, like red caterpillars (*Alice*), going slowly out of their gallery, Headlam and I went boldly down and mingled with the Peers.

One thing I had forgotten. When the procession was going out, the Choir door became inconveniently crowded. Esher[13] threw a line of guardsmen across the East of the Choir stalls, which held up the peers. The peeresses nearest spent the time in talking to the guardsmen and making little jokes. When the choir was cleared, the cordon was withdrawn and the peers let loose.

I saw Eddy Cadogan[14], with the armlet of a steward. Then a nice family group of St Germans – he like a rather tipsy sailor! But Eliot[15] looked very elegant, and a little boy dressed as a page – my future pupil. Then I met Elliot (Sir J.) of the Agricultural Office and bantered him on not wearing his insignia. Then we went down nave and into Annexe. This, hung with tapestries and trophies of arms, was *most* successful – and so too outside, though I confess I thought the design a poor one and the verisimilitude of age the best part of it. It was simply a great hall inside with rows of pillars. People sate waiting for carriages – an absurd group of peers and peeresses hob-nobbing over sandwiches, like almsmen and almswomen, with Lady Sligo in the midst, all looking rather wrinkled and tired in the daylight. Here I met Robert Collins who had sent off his Duchess[16] and now waited like a little noticing philosopher looking coolly about. We ought not of course to have been in any of these places, but by dint of simply walking there in an unconcerned way were not stopped. Here I met Esher and congratulated him. It was so refreshing to talk to one person who in spite of all his robes etc. was exactly as simple and natural as any day. He laid his hand on my arms and said impressively that it *was* a relief – but that he *knew*, as far as prescience was possible in human affairs, that it *would* go perfectly. They had spared *no* pains and had gone on till it was perfect.

Here we saw the finest sight of all, shown me by Headlam. From the *annexe*, the view through the black weather-mouldered door

---

[13] Reginald Brett, second Viscount Esher, who later collaborated with A.C.B. in editing Queen Victoria's letters.
[14] The elder of the two Cadogan boys, sons of the Viceroy of Ireland, in A.C.B.'s House.
[15] Lord Eliot, in his third year at Eton, son of the fourth Earl of St. Germans.
[16] The Duchess of Albany. Sir Robert Collins was her equerry.

(which tho' really external, was now inside *annexe*): first, the nave arches, then the screen, very black, with the glimmering arch beneath, and then the blaze of light above, with the stately figures moving about – the whole in a kind of golden mist – it was almost incredibly beautiful.

The only feeling was that it *was* theatrical, or like one of the old steel-engravings of a great court ceremony. One felt actually inclined to say that the architecture was very clever but wrong – and unsubstantial.

Two or three other little points I mention just as they occur to me. As I was wandering about with Headlam, we found two black fierce men, of the suite of Nas Mahommen I believe, sitting mute in a corner, rather gorgeously habited, except that one of them, otherwise dressed in cloths of good, had a large white Homburg hat on his knee. Sir W. Laurier, in his blue Michael and George robes, was most splendid – like a cardinal – he moved and spoke so gracefully and simply – one of the finest figures there. Remember the little red-faced peer, with a coronet down over his ears, sitting and kicking a white leg on the arm of the King's Recognit chair.

I am told that the King's answers were very finely given, and that he looked sternly and grimly about him, not at all complacently. The Queen bowing to him and his bow back were very impressive. In fact he is a good actor – if there were only a little more real kingliness about him! The various banners of England and Scotland etc. looked well. They were held outside the choir door by the poor Cinque Port Barons, who were deprived of their privilege of canopy.

M.B. had an odd adventure. When she got to her place and was sitting there, Reggie Lister came to her and said '*Would* you mind moving from here, Mrs Benson. We have to put some of the foreign suites in here.' She replied that she did not much wish to move. He replied that it was his chief's orders. So she moved and was shown to another place, rather better. When she went out, R.L. hurriedly showed a lady to her place and said, 'There, that will be all right.' M.B. found that she was sitting in the Royal Chaplain's seats (who by the way were very oddly habited in red mantles buttoned at the neck). Presently Johnnie Ellison[17] came up to take his place, but M.B. sturdily refused to move again. It was rather a shabby trick of R.L.

Randall said that he spent an hour on Friday in the King's dressing-room at Buckingham Palace trying on all his robes. When they had put them on, the Queen burst in – 'Oh, I must look at you, I must see what it looks like.' He said they were so friendly and jolly together – so unlike what is usually supposed – not at all stately, rather like what good-natured *farmer* sort of folk would have said and done – but very hearty and cheerful and domestic all the same.

I got out about 3.30 and went to Barton St., where they were at lunch – very hungry and tired – but revived as soon as I had taken off my tight robes and shoes. I went off to club to read and smoke. Coming back down Whitehall it was pleasant to see the crowds. They were serious, interested, not amused, no rowdiness, just silently parading. I was in a hansom and we had to go at a fool's pace. There was a sea of heads with a distant hansom wading through. But the order and gravity were very nice; and there has been no disorder at all.

When I turned into Barton St, about a dozen *gamins* had made up a game of cricket in the street, coats for wickets, and were gravely playing as if there was nothing else to do and the street belonged to them. (I could not make out how some of the people got in to the Coronation. Just below me were two very bourgeois people in morning dress, like a tradesman and wife, who ate peppermints and looked horribly out of place. But I fancy that there were many vacant places and people were almost compelled to come in.)

[Volume 16, pp.86–120]

---

[17] The Rev. J. H. J. Ellison, Vicar of Windsor, one of Randall Davidson's chaplains.

VI

◇

He relaxes in Norfolk and experiences a drive in a motor-car

Rarely did a summer pass by, in these days, without Arthur joining a family party with the Donaldsons. Stuart Donaldson was about ten years Arthur's senior, but they were colleagues for most of their lives; first, as Eton housemasters, and then – when Donaldson became Master of Magdalene College, Cambridge in 1903 – he procured for Arthur a Fellowship there in the following year. In 1915, on Donaldson's death, Arthur succeeded him as Master of Magdalene.

Sometimes they would meet for shooting-parties at the Scottish estate at Dunskey in Wigtownshire. On other occasions there would be gatherings at Aylsham in Norfolk. In September 1902, shortly after Donaldson's marriage to Lady Albinia Hobart-Hampden, Arthur joined a typical family party, presided over by Lady Donaldson (who was devoted to Arthur) and her sister, Baroness von Brandt. Stuart and Lady 'Alba', with their baby daughter, were there; also their cousins, Algy and May Lawley. The party was augmented, from time to time, by other Eton colleagues, and Mary Benson herself came for a few days. They explored the Broads; they visited various distinguished neighbours; and at Ditchingham, where they went for a shooting expedition, Arthur was introduced to the writer, Rider Haggard. This particular visit was notable for his first experience of driving in a motor-car. As they flew through

Norwich, with heads turning to look at them in envy and admiration, Arthur felt it was all 'like a dream'.

I read stupidly all up to town, papers and ephemeralities. Looked out a little, with a pang, at the quiet lanes near Three Bridges where I bicycled so short a time ago. To London Bridge, and then to Liverpool St. The stations horribly crowded and the train late. Somehow the moving throng across London Bridge, of clerks coming back to work after dinner, fascinated me strangely. How apathetic the Englishman looks – neither miserable nor happy – he just walks along. The younger men talk and smile a little, and the older men look tired: but I can easily conceive a foreigner thinking them dull, hard, proud and insolent. But I felt more than this. To see this huge cataract of life, to reflect that a percentage of them will die within the year – what all their lives mean – it seems such a poor thing – and yet I suppose they are 'dear to God' if not to anyone else.

I went through Essex, by Ipswich, and changed at Norwich. I was mostly alone, for which I was dully grateful, and read, with a worm at my heart. How stupid one is! At Norwich I was told by a paper-boy there were ladies calling for me. I couldn't find them. I wrote letters in pencil. Got to Aylsham and found the ladies were Lady Alba – who looks well after her illness – and Mrs Lawley. St Clair[1] and Stuart Donaldson were there, having bicycled. We walked up.

Aylsham is a very pleasant little town of warm red-brick houses, with rather a foreign look. It looks clean, wholesome and comfortable. There are many houses which I wish to inhabit, of course. We walked about a little. The Rectory lies at the further end of the town, in a nice glebe and garden under the Church. A good house and well kept. Nice shrubs and trees and flowers.

---

[1] St Clair Donaldson, brother of Stuart, later Archbishop of Brisbane and Bishop of Salisbury.

There is a fine dining-room with white pillars and it is altogether a good substantial house. The Church is long and low, a large grey flint building, low-pitched roof – transepts and aisles, with a very fine tower. The party consists of Stuart and Alba, the Baroness, Lady Donaldson, St Clair; and Mrs Lawley who has been taking a cure and is rather knocked up. The baby is a fine tranquil child, fond of music, and is much worshipped and adored. I do not think I have the maternal instinct – but I find myself wondering what the grave eyes see and what the little brain thinks of. We dined very cheerfully and pleasantly.

The next day was Sunday and we all went to Church. It is a fine spacious Church, carefully kept and with an air of wealth. Canon Hoare is a rich Evangelical. There was a large congregation of a rather well-to-do kind. A choir, but not surpliced, of men, boys and women, sang briskly – the organ was smartly played. Some nice chants and hymns which I had never heard before. Some windows of the kind which Kempe would detest and I love; laborious, of screaming or rich tints, affected – but somehow showing love and care.

After lunch, we walked out to Blickling. Since Lady Lothian's death it has been kept up elaborately – twenty gardeners – but no one admitted to the house. One Bertram Talbot, a thick-set young man, a cousin of Lady Lothian, lives there, as agent, but more as a kind of gentlemanly policeman, to keep everyone out – even the Meyricks at the vicarage who have been in and out for twenty years, can't get in there now. I once met Lady Lothian at Lord Brownlow's house, at lunch. She was talking about the marriage of Jenkinson (University Librarian) and Miss Whetton. She said, 'I always think it is so bad for two of a trade to marry – and particularly tiresome when two *teaching* people get together.' Harry Cust, with malignant glee, said 'Well, aunt, you *have* put your foot in it.' Lady L. smiled vaguely, looked at me, perceiving that I was in question, and said sweetly 'Oh, of course I didn't mean University Dons, Mr Benson – that's quite another thing. I was thinking of schoolmasters.'

The road comes suddenly upon the house, which lies not in the centre of its park, but at the extreme corner, like many of the great houses. You look up about 100 yards, through yew hedges, very splendid and velvety, past a range of great outbuildings on each side, looking like a College Court, at the front, with its lead-capped turrets and balustraded mullions. The effect is somehow not absolutely satisfactory. In the first place it looks a little as if it were sinking into the ground – it has a moat – and in the second place it is either too orante or not ornate enough.

We walked boldly round and saw the great gardens. At the back stretches away a huge fern-clad park, but it looked sad and deserted, tho' the gardens are all kept up. Vanity of vanities!

Then we went to the Church. There is a fine marble monument by Watts to Lord Lothian. The angels are beautiful at head and feet, looking wistful and yet serene. The figure is a fine one, but the hair and beard too flamboyant. He wore his hair like *Dickens*, I suppose, and this is not adapted for marble. The drapery is very unconventional, and the result is that though it is beautiful, it looks rather as if he had been tossed in a blanket and considerably rumpled. There was a handsome parson, Mr Meyrick Wood, in the church – and his wife – a Miss Meyrick – very pretty and nice. He seemed to know nothing about the church or monuments. We went into the Rectory, a fine house, but dark, ill-kept and second rate. Saw old Canon Meyrick, who sate in a little hot study, with a *fire* (Therm. outside at 70) waiting for the end. He suffers from his throat. His old well-worn books in the shelves; by him a few papers and a cup and plate. He was chaplain to Christopher Wordsworth in '69, with my father, and I remember him at Riseholme.[2] His hair and beard are like floss silk. He was interested to see me, but it made me low-spirited to think of him fading away. He will never leave the house again. We dined pleasantly. Mr Cole, the *locum tenens* came – a nice man but very nervous. He is assistant and curate to Garnier of Quidenham. We talked afterwards about wealth and the duty of tithe. He quoted 'Corban'

---

[2] The palace of the Bishop of Lincoln. E. W. Benson was Chancellor of Lincoln from 1873 to 1877.

aptly [Mark, 7, 11]. He called all the ladies Mrs Donaldson with impartial politeness, hoping to be right for once, I suppose.

Monday, we shot: the keeper is a farmer. We saw a great many birds and went over and over the same ground. But we did not shoot very well, and had no dog – got 8 brace and lost 3 brace of dead birds. Lunched in the farm – a nice glazed cupboard let into the wall. The country pleasant, with red brick and red tiled houses – nice oak avenues, meadows and woods – not exciting but pleasant. Algy Lawley arrived, full of humour and geniality, but white. I could not help laughing when Mrs Lawley said something about Harrogate, he leant forwards and said with extreme politeness. 'So you have been to Harrogate, have you?'

I have been reading the life of Lord Shaftesbury – a melancholy life somehow. But he did great services without much satisfaction. One story amuses me: after he became Lord Shaftesbury, he took a prominent part in some philanthropic scheme. An American paper, commenting on this, wrote: 'And who is Lord Shaftesbury? Who is this mushroom philanthropist who has sprung up in a single night, with this intense affected interest in the matter? Where has he been hitherto? Where was he skulking when Lord Ashley was fighting the same battle single-handed?'[3]

On *Tuesday* we went off, with Lady Alba in a donkey chair, to see Bolwich, in the morning. As we went over the bridge, we passed Lord Buxton on a bicycle, and shortly after, Birkbeck. As we came to the gate, a trap with two Miss Birkbecks drove swiftly out. I said that Mr B. had evidently rushed to the Post Office and telegraphed to Bolwich that the Donaldsons were bearing down in full force – *sauve qui peut*! Mrs Lawley at once charged the bewildered Miss B's with this. They drove on, but presently Miss Amy came back to entertain us. She is a pretty and interesting girl. She has, after long struggling, obtained her wish to study the piano in the R.C. of Music and lives alone in town. She told me that it

---

[3] Anthony Ashley Cooper, styled Lord Ashley in 1811, succeeded to the Earldom of Shaftesbury in 1851.

was far more delightful than even she had anticipated. She is very independent and finds Bolwich very dull, and wants to become a professional teacher; but thinking it might be disagreeable in England, wishes to go out to South Africa. She loves Parratt, of course, and Hubert Parry.

I was much interested in this pretty eager girl, with her dark complexion and handsome eyes, with sudden pallors. Not so in her mother, a sister of Henry Lee Warner, a 'weariful wife', ugly, voluble, tiresome, who loves archaeology and has arranged a huge picnic to see a castle. *That* is not the way to see a place. There was a dim woman there, Miss Dent, who sate in a chair and appeared at intervals to be asking where she was and who everyone might be. We walked in the sweet garden with its yew hedges, the cool clear lake among reeds. The garden is bounded by a stream and beyond melts into woodland. A corner, where a green alley lined with flowers came down opposite a great beech, will stay in my mind.

St Clair had gone off to Barningham to lunch with the Simpsons. After a quiet lunch at home, Stuart and I set off on bicycles to pick him up and to go on to Cley. We rode by Blickling and pleasant farmlands with red houses, and got to Barningham. The park very pretty, but the road ill-kept. It is a very fine tall Tudor house, with curious double dormer windows. As we drew up to the front we saw a party sitting out on a terrace. Men in light coats and brightly dressed females – the sort of group that sends my heart into my boots – but towed in the wake of Stuart's breezy self-possession, we strode in. Frank Simpson came out to meet us. I used to know him very well in the old Tan days[4]. He left Eton the year I went as a master. He was a delightful wholesome, good-humoured boy, in whom Howard Sturgis[5] endeavoured vainly to cultivate a taste for Botticelli. He has done *nothing* since, owning a brewery.... He is a little ashamed of his indolence, I think. He would have made such a good officer, clergyman or even school master that I cannot help feeling it a waste.

---

[4] A reference to reading-parties at Tan-yr-allt, near Portmadoc.
[5] The joint lease-holder of Tan, with A. C. Ainger; one of A.C.B.'s close friends of long standing.

Norfolk: a drive in a motor-car

I didn't much care for his mother who seemed superior. St Clair appeared to be giving them a kind of drawing-room lecture, but he was only 'putting' a golf ball. Miss Simpson, a pretty young lady, brought us out huge peaches – but I felt as if I were biting into a baby's skull. Simpson's uncle, a boring old man, with a notebook full of very unimportant and inaccurate information, plied me with questions about an inscription on a bell which he could not remember. We saw the house – not big, but very nice – a fine long drawing room, of rococo Gothic and a good staircase; a few pictures. The house is only taken on lease from one Mott, an odd rich man who lives in town in lodgings and clubs.

This easy, lazy, gentle life is rather perplexing. It looks so beautiful and tranquil, but it seems unfair and unfruitful. The boaring uncle took us to the Church, half in ruins – the tower empty, and an odd little stuffy choir used for services. Under the screen is a terrible vault, with long niches, like ovens, for coffins; those occupied closed at the mouth with slabs, where several Motts repose. The smell was awful and penetrating and I nosed Motts, like Hamlet, in the lobby, and I was glad to get out. We rode on, but the rain began to pelt. Saw a nice red house with good porch, at Plumstead, and giving up Cley, made our way home. Walked by workhouse in evening.

Wednesday. We shot beyond Harvey's farm – 13½ brace – we shot well. A nice piece of broken ground, with self-sown birches and firs, deep in ling, which – warmed by the sun – sent out a sweet smell. We lunched in a lonely farmyard, with a byre, with odd brick gateposts. I shot a hare, which fell into a ditch and wailed lamentably. Poor innocent creature! I felt a devil; the murder was soon over, and the draggled body put away. Childers[6] arrived and walked to Blickling with May (Lawley).

Thursday, September 4. A delicious day. We went off early and caught 9.50 train to Wroxham. Here a difficulty occurred. We

---

[6] H. R. E. Childers, a close friend both at Eton and King's.

were told we might have a steam-launch, and by going to get it, lost the wherry we had provisionally engaged. Stuart was justly annoyed and spoke with tempered indignation to an old man like a clergyman with a chin beard. However we were at last accommodated with a big roomy sailing-boat and sate round. Miss Buxton was with us (S.A.D., St. Clair, May, Algy, Childers and John the footman). We had books and papers and jested innocently.

We sailed slowly down the Bure, tacking from side to side. This broad rushy river, with the great flat on every side, with the low distant rising-ground, with alder clumps and dykes, and opening into still sheets of water on every side, was extraordinarily beautiful. Much meadow-sweet and hoosestrife and valerian. But there were many – too many – people about. The river winds very much, and it is beautiful to see ahead of you apparently in the fields the white graceful sails of a huge wherry (a wherry is not a row-boat, but a big, broad sailing-boat) moving silently along. We passed many happy parties – fathers with their boys, under-graduates etc. The dirty flannels and tumbled hair, unbrushed after bathing, betrayed the campers-out. The undergraduate, sullen, conscious, puffing his pipe, is a disagreeable sort of creature, I think.

A nasty regatta was going on at Horning, the bank crowded and boats tacking as they raced. It was more still and silent as we tacked briskly up the creek to Ranworth; a man was mowing sedges underneath a broken pumping-mill which made a pleasant picture. We landed on a quay, covered with sedge-stacks. A little boy proffered me 'beans, peas, potatoes, apples and plums'. Then we walked up to Ranworth Church, by a pleasant thatched house in a trim garden. The bare high flint tower is impressive. It is being restored, with care and love. The great painted screen is fine, but few people seem to realise that it must have been hideous when new and that age is *the* toning grace. The most interesting thing there was an old pre-Reformation chanting-desk, with a hideous painted eagle, and an old 'Gloria' with musical notation painted on the upper part for the choir to sing from. The foot worm-eaten.

Norfolk: a drive in a motor-car

We rambled about a little grassy acre, and came back to lunch at the boat; a rich lunch of cold meats, fruits and jellies. Then we got slowly under way and went on to a ruined abbey – St Bene't-at-holm – which sent an abbot to the House of Lords, and the Bishop of Norwich *still* sits as abbot of this place. It lies in a great green marshy flat on a low island. The gate-house is fairly intact, with a groined roof, but a huge brick pumping-mill has been built in it – very incongruous. The old precinct-wall is visible, and part of the nave and transept of the church among grassy tumbled mounds. It must have been a very lonely place. The two odd ivy-grown towers of S. Waltham – and many other grey towers – visible far off over the green flat. The barn of a farm close by is the chapel of the hospital.

We embarked again, the wind dropping every moment, and a golden light falling over the lazy ripples and reeds. The sedge in a high wind, such as we had in the morning, is the most delicious thing both to see and hear. We got a little tired, I think, but talked and jested. I should have liked a little more serious feeling talk, I think – more in tune – but perhaps impossible for so big a party (this sounds horribly priggish; but I don't mean it so. What I mean is that all sorts of little gentle thoughts hovered about, and yet one could not speak of them, tho' probably everyone else was feeling the same). There is a sadness about so bright, sweet and happy a day fading slowly to evening. One has not too many of such days. Horning Church tower stood up among its dark trees like an old engraving.

We saw an odd little drama here on returning. A stout lady had just returned from fishing, with one stiff silvery dace in a net. She hobbled to the house with some wraps, and a black cat took advantage of her absence to steal the dace and walk swiftly off with it. The lady returned; the cat went off round a shed; but we could see both; and to see the cat glaring with the dace in its mouth, and the fat lady hunting in an agonised way in all directions for the fish was very funny. She went sadly off at last, thinking I suppose that the dace had revived and skipt away.

Then the wind dropped; and we had to row with sweeps. This

84

was disgusting drudgery, and came at the end of so sweet a day, and just when everything was at its very best. A merry party of Birkbecks went past in a steamer, and knowing Miss Buxton, screamed out with full mouths that they were having tea. 'Then you are very greedy!' said Miss B. severely; and was greeted by derisive cheers. The silhouette on the top of the cabin, a tall slim girl with blowing hair, being helped to tea by slender handsome brothers was very nice. We dragged slowly on – mocked at by silent sleepy fishermen, and by a huge stout man on a launch going down stream, whose head slowly revolved to watch us.

We determined at last to quit the boat; we plunged into a quiet mere, Stalhouse?, belonging to the Cators, with a rustic tea-house among the trees. Got on shore and through green lanes and quiet villages, hurried to Stalhouse station, leaving poor John with the baggage. I walked with Miss Buxton and had a delightful talk. She is simple, interesting and fresh. Passed a charming park, with long grass like velvet under the trees in the evening light. We caught the train and rumbled home, a merry tired party. Miss Buxton, opposite me, a charming figure.

The young man who steered us was a nice willing fellow. I think he must have felt he had treated us badly and wanted to make up.

I can't understand the conformation of this country – its extreme flatness, rising a few inches straight from the water's edge. I think it must have been pushed up by volcanic pressure a little, and the soil is the marsh bottom, the river the deeper channels, the Broads the deeper pools. But it is all rather mysterious. It gave me a sense of seclusion to look from the populous river into the green flat, with its waving sedge and alder thickets.

As we got home a little group of Salvation Army people were singing and preaching in front of the house; their plan is to sing and play alternate verses; then someone speaks. I listened through my bedroom window. It seemed to me very poor. It was all 'Come to Jesus and be saved' and gratitude for what he had done for us – but it didn't say what you were to do afterwards – go around and sing hymns, I suppose. That is all very well as long as very few people do it – but a system which would extinguish the life of the world if it became universal is surely on the wrong track. The men only spoke, quite continuously and rather eloquently. The soft voices of the women were audible occasionally 'Yes, yes!' 'Do, Lord!' – 'Yes, it is so, Alleluia'. It was odd to see this in the quiet dusty street. No one looked on or listened – no hostility but not the faintest interest either . . .

Saturday, September 6. We started about 12 bicycling, through pleasant lanes to Cawston. On the way passed a new house, built by a South African millionaire called *Cawston* who has settled here to be Cawston of Cawston. A large hamlet of nice redbrick houses with Elizabethan gables – over all a huge stone ashlar tower, very dignified – unfinished – no parapet or pinnacles – pierced with a few little quatrefoil windows to light the staircases, like patches on a Caroline court beauty's face. The Church very large and noble: a great chestnut roof, transepts, fearfully uncomfortable little sitting-benches, but all pretty well-kept. The Rectory belongs to Pembroke, Cambridge – £1000 a year – Mr Marsh, a tiresome old parson, who came jawing about, has been there fifty years. On the warm lead roof sate hundreds of martins gathering for their voyage oversea. We toiled up the tower, only to find the trapdoor shut. The tower is huge, like a cathedral – and all built for the glory of God, as there can never have been more than a hamlet here.

Then on to Heydon. We went to the Grange – Sir Edward Bulwer – for luncheon. He is an old soldier, Crimea and Mutiny, and then Permanent Under-Secretary at the War Office – a courteous old man, in feeble health, with a weary warrior sort of face – cousin of the Lyttons. The Grange – a farmhouse, with low pleasant rooms and a pretty trim garden – very livable. There was a Miss Bulwer at lunch – buxom and kind – an old General Elrington, 84 years old and very spry, riding a little bicycle afterwards. A dumb sad lady who sate next me, and two jolly little boys, Nugents, who are to go to Eton, barelegged and sandalled. Lunch was not unpleasant and I pumped Sir E. about Lord Lothian. It is a sad story. He was a young man of high promise – a double first at Oxford – went out with Dalhousie to India on his staff, got a sunstroke and died at 40, having long been an invalid. His brother, the Secretary for Scotland, rather an invalid too. *His* eldest son, a delightful, gentle, intelligent Eton boy killed out shooting in India – and the present Marquis a lunatic. Here is a cheerful tale!

After lunch we went to see the Church – very neat and trim, with Bulwer monuments … Into the Hall Park, by a great gate with urns atop, and a grove of sycamores – shimmering turf beyond. The Hall a fine Elizabethan place, very large, but looking neglected – let for years, as the General has a place elsewhere. The present tenant a Managing Director of Collieries, who comes for shooting. He came out upon us – a man like a butler, very fresh and acute – not a gentleman. He took us back – he had a young officer with him, a cub who had come back from South Africa. A fine panelled hall. Here he introduced us to a feeble bearded man, Professor something, whose attempts at conversation were fitful and his bearing highly inadequate. The pictures plentiful and good. A fine one of G. Villiers, Duke of Buckingham, *asleep*. They said he could only be painted by stealth; and on this occasion he was drunk – all stuff! Many Pastons and Bulwers, with fat faces like ripe plums. The Hall panelled with Cromwellian Ironsides and hung with Morions. We went out at the back – stately but neglected – grass in the walks, hedges straggling. Sir Edward looked sadly about, and said 'I was born here – you can't think how I love the place.'

It is heavily mortgaged; and it is rather sad to think of it let to a Colliery Manager! Fine avenues of oaks to Cawston and Salle. We went off at last; and rode to Salle – caught up the Colliery party in a waggonette … We rode on to see an extraordinary church with two towers recently built by Elwin, Editor of *Quarterly Review* – designed by himself. Hideous in the extreme– towers set lozenge-wise to the Church, all thick where it ought to be thin, and thin where it ought to be thick. I never saw a more pathetic place. It must have cost £50,000 and is designed in a sort of bastard Gothic, part French, part Early Victorian. Munich or Bruges glass. Very carefully furnished within: chairs, wood pavement – all perfect, and all ugly; but it is *well* done, and age will improve all good faithful work. A grim handsome priest in a cassock gave us short answers and seemed to wish us away.

So we went; back through Cawston. I shall always think of Cawston as I saw it then – standing up very square and sober over sycamores and red roofs, gilt by evening light. The swallows flying all about it like swarming bees, and settled in hundreds on the steep under-sill of the louvre windows – age and youth – experience and hope!

Sunday. Today we went to Church – a nice sober service cheerfully sung. Stuart preached a good sermon and Mr Cole read the prayers sadly. The lessons read by a solicitor, with a majestic and princely aspect, dressed for public life in frock coat and patent leather boots. The brothers Talbot came to lunch, heavy-faced young men, but amiable. But how few interesting, lively, strange people one meets – conversation instead of being a pleasure is a dreary exercise. In the afternoon sate under cedar and walked – Childers, St Clair and I – to Ingworth, through meadows at first. Discussed the social position of the clergy. I believe that the *general* level is high. Vicarages everywhere look comfortable, and I believe that though the old church pluralists were great men enough, the curate of a non-resident vicar was often a very boorish poverty-stricken man, e.g. I am sure that the condition of such a household as Amos Barton's in G. Eliot is an exception now.

Tea and some baby-worship. Miss Donaldson is a tranquil, good-humoured child, fond of music and capable. But I don't think babies are interesting at that stage – like little guinea-pigs – though the ladies gaze with large-eyed wonder and prattle away, proud of winning a smile. Strolled with M.B. on the turf and smoked a little – very pleasant.

September 11. We have escaped today from Mrs Buxton's Archaeological Expedition – and as it is cold and grey, with occasional sprinkles of rain, we are glad. The idea of driving about with thirty people whom one doesn't know in waggonettes from

Norfolk: a drive in a motor-car

Tudor House to Tudor House, and being lectured there by horribly intelligent and well regulated persons is detestable. Yesterday we had a fairly pleasant day – that was all that could be said. We were a very large party (S.A.D, St Clair, Fred Donaldson[7], Sir J.Clark, Lady C., Lady Alba, M.B., Miss Carr, 3 Fred Donald children – and last of all two Miss Cowpers, pleasant sturdy girls, Lady Donaldson's nieces). We had a good steamlaunch, only just not big enough, as there was no circulation possible, and we sate like hens, where we first found ourselves. Consequently the women got all stuck in the forepart, the men in the centre and the children at the stern. I drifted in among the women for a bit. M.B. began to tell a story of a lady to whom she had sent a confidential letter who had at once sent it on – adding 'but she was a Christian Scientist'. I said 'Oh, well' and became aware that something was wrong. Lady Alba plunged gallantly into a long and amusing account of an experience of being spoken rudely to by an English Abbé in Italy in the train, who she afterwards met at the Villa Medici at lunch. I tried to pull the subject out of the fire, by turning someone else on, like the cat and the monkey. But it wouldn't do. I afterwards heard that Miss Carr was an ardent Christian Scientist – but she plunged into the subject later with M.B. and seemed to have taken no offence.

We crept gently on – but the day was not pleasant. There was a cool wind, with a sort of hot background to it – and it was grey and uninviting. We went into Wroxham Broad and then on to S.Waltham Broad, where I saw grebes. Somehow it didn't move me. I was 'remote, unfriended, melancholy, slow'.

Here we lunched in the little saloon, I not wisely; then we determined to return, and went back in sprinkling rain. The others to the train – St Clair and I bicycled back; tried to go slow but failed. This somehow a melancholy day. . . .

We were to start early on Friday for Ditchingham, where I was invited by the Carrs. We made a hasty breakfast and the motor came hissing and snorting to the door. Lady Donaldson very

---

7 Sir Frederick Donaldson, later drowned in the same ship as Lord Kitchener.

affectionate,,and rather alarmed about the cold. She was dreadfully distressed about the thinness of my cloak and wanted me to wear a shawl. 'You are precious, you know, to me as well as to others.' Said good-bye, and went off with a bound – Stuart, Lady Alba, Miss Carr – a rather prim gentle lady of about forty, who has been staying with the Donaldsons, a bosom friend of Lady A's – and myself. We ran very pleasantly along by Bolwich and the wellknown lanes; then through the great still woods of Stratton Strawless – the huge ugly barrack of the house looking comfortable enough, where Birkbeck lives. . . . Certainly a motor is delightful; I felt inclined to say like Dr Johnson that there could be few pleasures greater. Through St Faith's and then Norwich, smoking and steaming, lay below us. A bad watery morning.

We tore through the streets. A fine glimpse of the huge spire over the houses, and one glance into the Close through the big gate. Many nice houses but smoke-blackened; horrible little courts, dark and smelly, under archways; flint-built churches innumerable. We were detained by a tyre accident. The brake had jammed and planed a long string off. Soon remedied, and we tore on again. Passed through a rich-looking suburb, and then on towards Ditchingham – Bixley Hall, once Lord Rosebery's – Brooke House, a place like Terling in a park, belonging to Lord Canterbury, who lives in a small house at Seething and drinks with his coachman. Then to Ditchingham – some delightful houses left and right, particularly Hevingham Hall, like Tremans[8].

We met Willy Carr in the drive – we were very late – so sent the ladies to the house, worked the car round, making a horrible mess like a maltese cross on grass and gravel and scummy pools – and on to Ditchingham House, where Rider Haggard lives. He and Willy Carr run their shooting together.

Old Mr W. Carr is a Yorkshireman descended from the Carrs of Stackhouse by Settle. He began as a surgeon, but was taken up by a maternal uncle, Mr Greenwood of Gomersal, who practically

---

[8] The Benson home, recently acquired on a tenancy from Mrs Hardy of Horsted Keynes. The reference to Terling is to the country seat of Lord Rayleigh, who, by his marriage to Evelyn Balfour, became a relation of the Bensons and Sidgwicks.

adopted him, left him Gomersal and £70,000. He married a Miss Whitaker with £30,000 (all this he told me) and is now a very rich man. He bought Ditchingham in 1884. He is a distant cousin of ours – I think he was my mother's third cousin, once removed – thro' the Carrs of Bolton – also distantly related to my father through the Smiths of Greare House.

We got out at Ditchingham House, a nice trim brick-built house. Rider Haggard appeared, tall, stout, amiable. He is pale with a short beard and rather shambles as he walks; dressed in a large pale coat and gaiters. He seemed both overworked and ill. Various women and smart young men lounged around.

Willy Carr is a small neat handsome man, youthful complexion and hard grey eyes – very shy. He married Miss Bright, daughter of Bright, Master of Univ. Coll., Oxford, the day he took his degree – and tho' he is younger than me, he has a fourteen-year old daughter.

With us came one Christian, a mining engineer in Cyprus. Haggard confided to me that from various indications in old books he was sure that Cyprus was rich in *mines*. He quoted the Odyssey with gusto (old Mr Carr tells me that Haggard is not a well-informed man, but can 'butter his knowledge very thin and make it go a long way') – and it was he who financed Christian. 'Cyprus = copper, you see', he added. They have found out old workings, made by a pygmy race – and he hopes they will be successful eventually. Meantime they are not.

A nice keeper, like a clergyman, and two of the handsomest boys to beat I have ever seen – in different ways. One roguish, English, with a perpetual smile and large white teeth – a common country boy, but of extraordinarily graceful carriage. Whatever he did looked well. The other, the keeper's son, could have been dressed up to make a really beautiful woman. Also a young soldier, a hussar, who carried my cartridges; had been through Ladysmith and thrice wounded – very smart and modest. He is going back as Sergeant Instructor on £240 a year. He wouldn't talk of his experiences.

We went round pretty country overlooking Bungay, where

Norfolk: a drive in a motor-car

Clay prints my books; far in the flat the tower of Beccles. Haggard is a great farmer and writes books about it. I never saw so well-farmed a place. He gets just a small return, he says. The property is his wife's. There were few birds, and I began badly but afterwards shot well (5 out of 17 brace). Haggard lounged, smiled, talked – but seemed tired and fell into long silences waking up to amiable smiles. I told him how familiar his portrait was to me – he gave it to Gosse[9] – he asked whether I thought it good, and seemed to regret having given it away.

We lunched well in a cartshed – Haggard very genial. He told us of his strange experiences in touring about inspecting agriculture (he is hard at work writing a book on Rural England): a strange drunken farmer's where he stayed, where you could get anything to drink and nothing to eat; bad eggs etc. 'The fact is, Mr Haggard, I'm a very temperate *eater*.' Christian told us of his horrible adventures boring a hole to let the water out of a submerged mine on a mountain side. They bored from below and never knew when it might break out on them. It *did* break out, but they got away in time, down a shaft 3 feet high.

After lunch, round fields by a House of Mercy and Ditchingham Church. Here I shot a fine rocheting shot which fell into the Convent orchard. Haggard more and more tired. Walked homewords. Ditchingham Park is very beautiful – well timbered with a long lake full of duck. The house a mellow Queen Anne front, white-casemented on a rising ground, with great cedars by it. Went into a big hall, with portraits – Mr Carr of Bolton etc. Old Mr Carr came out, a regular old Yorkshireman, stout, lame, a small tough man – with a keen face and a shaved upper lip; very hospitable; gave us tea and talked about the estate – he is very deaf.

I had a delightful room, big and comfortable – a regular old country-house room, with a dressing-room opening out of it. A nervous genial butler. Changed slowly and read *Pride and Prejudice*. The whole feeling of the place was like Miss Austen. Down to dinner. Young Mrs Carr a pleasant wry lady; old Mrs Carr like a

---

9 Edmund Gosse, A.C.B.'s closest friend, at that stage, in the literary world.

very benevolent and nervous ghost – very frail, large-eyed and nervously twitchy. She is devoted to her husband, and he treated her nicely, rallying her good-naturedly – 'We daren't leave Mrs Carr at home', he said, 'because she is so mischievous – so we have to take her with us.' But he got by her in the drawing-room, and took her hand gently when no one was looking.

A good dinner – but Marsala only offered to drink. There were green claret-glasses and when I refused Marsala, the butler said to me 'What will you drink?' I said, 'claret – anything'. He said in a whisper 'There's no claret opened.' So I drank barley-water. Afterwards very fine old port. Mr Carr ate his dinner, smiled, didn't say much. Mrs W.Carr (junior) seemed shy. I took her in, but I found favour by praising Burge[10], not knowing her to be his sister-in-law. Willy rallied his father a good deal, and the old gentleman liked it. Willy is an interesting fellow. He got three Prize Essays, Lothian etc., at Oxford, and a first; he writes for the Dictionary of National Biography and is a barrister; has stood for Parliament; lives at the Hall Farm.

After dinner Mr Carr took me off and we had a long genealogical talk. He has great collection of interesting papers. He knew all about my relations and their exact fortunes. Seemed rather vexed that Mr Carr of Bolton had left so much to my grandmother. . . . He read the paper like a philosopher. Then we smoked in the Hall, and he gave me more information. Finally we could find no matches and he went and hunted in the dark – I could hear him tumble about – and conducted me to my bedroom. 'Here's your room – here's your dressing-room – all you want? Sleep well – you are welcome here, as one of the old stock!' I slept well, in a comfortable bed, the great cedar outside softly roaring in a strong S.W. wind.

September 13. I got up leisurely and found Mr Carr waiting. He showed me the Bedingfield arms in the windows, with their

---

[10] H.M.Burge, later Bishop of Southwark and Bishop of Oxford; at that time, Headmaster of Winchester.

alliances – also some MSS, *Horae*, Bibles etc. – I candidly don't care twopence for such things. Lady Alba rallied him and said 'Mary tells me you have lots of these things hidden all over the house.' 'Aha!', said Mr Carr, 'Yes, indeed – in holes and corners – like an old magpie, anywhere!' We breakfasted – Mrs Carr not there – the large light room with many windows rather painful.[11] Mr Carr consumed many slices of smoked ham and nothing else. He then made me write a little note on the family connections in the big record-book, where I was amused to see other letters of my own stuck, and then we went off shooting, driving by Hevingham Hall, out to a lonely high kind of plateau. The wind was keen and the sun bright.

Our first task was to walk up long wide pasture fields with thick hedges – a gun and a beater in each field so that for some time we were alone. There was nothing of any kind to shoot – but somehow, what with the bright sun, the flowers of the pasture, the green trees and hedges – the thistles rising softly, like wading men, out of the light brown grass, I fell into a mood of keen, conscious and elated happiness such as I have seldom known since I was a boy. It was all so fresh and sweet, so quiet and lonely, as we walked, like tiny insects in the chequered squares of the wide country-side. So small we must have seemed from above, so busy about nothing. But the peace and glee of the green unvisited land, with its hazel-shadowed lanes, its undisturbed woods – with the clouds flying over it, in a bright blue sky, came into my very soul; and I had a beautiful and happy hour, for which I thank God.

At one gate there was a pleasing sight. A circle of sheep standing round an old merry shepherd – one pushing against his knees to be petted while he pulled its silky ear. His dogs stood at a distance. He had a real old shepherd-crook (which I think Missionary Bishops ought to carry). He had a weatherbeaten face, all wrinkled with good temper and cold, rough, not ungraceful country clothes and a great flapping hat. He talked very pleasantly. 'I'll lead my sheep

---

[11] A.C.B. hated bright light – electric light at night, the sun shining in on him through glass in the morning.

out over yonder', he said, 'to be out of you gentlemen's way; and send you good sport', and so he took his hat off and went off smiling to himself.

In the middle of one of these fields lived a horse-dealer in a van, beside a lilied pool, who hired the meadows in summer and lived an odd free sort of life – looking at nothing round him, I suppose.

Sport was very poor. We only got 10 brace all day. Carr went off before lunch. We plunged down a green valley thro' a wood, and had a drive in the Park; then to the Hall and lunched in the Magistrate's room, a stiff sort of parlour, like the one at Terling. Then out again by Miss Lillett's cottage – found a few birds. I shot straight, but got little shooting; killed a poor turtle-dove. Came in 4.30 and changed; more papers – Mr Carr most genial – tea. While Mr Carr and I were sitting in the hall, not far from the front door, which had glass panes, there came a seedy frowsy parson and rang. Mr C. looked up: 'Oh, here's our Vicar, Scudamore, a very good fellow, but an awful bore – he is always coming and hanging about here. Don't take any notice of him. Look at this.' No one answered the bell, and Mr Scudamore stood looking in meekly upon us. At last after ten minutes we saw him fumbling at the bell again. Mr Carr went and opened it, and shook hands and introduced me. Mr Scudamore a shy-looking owlish man, overgrown with hair, badly dressed in dirty oily clothes – unbrushed and unkempt. Mr Carr said – sharply but good-humouredly and very courteously: 'Now, sir, what do you want of me?' Mr S. pulled papers out of his pocket and began asking Mr C. to support a candidate for some village official post – relieving officer. 'Impossible', said Mr C., 'It's all settled. Nussey is to have it!' 'But won't you look at these papers, Mr Carr?' 'No I won't. I have made up my mind, and that's a troublesome thing to do, and maybe I should have to change it.' He pushed the papers away, and Mr Scudamore's extended hand with them. 'But there are to be *two* officers, Mr Carr.' 'And pray who told you that?' 'The Magistrate's Clerk, I think.' 'Well, it's under discussion.' 'Now, Mr Carr, do get my man the other place. He is a good honest fellow and wants it. I know you can do what you like with the Board.' Mr Carr, much mollified: 'Well, I don't know about that. Here, you can put your papers down *there*', indicating a place on the table, '*there*, please, precisely – well, I daresay I can do something for your man, if it's not Prescott – hey? Prescott's a rogue. And now, Scudamore, go away – I am engaged with Mr Benson and he is just leaving us. Here, go and have some tea with Mrs Carr – that door', aside to me in a loud voice, long before the hapless man had got out of the room, 'He's an awful bore, Scudamore – look at this.'

Then we went in to tea. Mrs Carr very birdlike and timid. The motor was late, but we took it tranquilly. Then we had a delicious run back. The lamps were lit in Norwich, and we tore through the narrow winding streets. It was like a dream to flash into the centre of a busy peopled town, to speak to no one and yet pass so close – and we must have seemed mysterious passengers too, sweeping in and out again. A good many people stopped to look at us. Then through the grey wolds and woods of S. Strawless. The moon rose, and when we got to Aylsham, the Church tower stood out in incredible beauty, tipped with gold, a few clouds sailing in a dark sky.

[Volume 17, pp.60–74; Volume 18, pp. 1–35]

VII

◇

He is the guest of his Head Master at Baron's Down

In *Memories and Friends*, his last book of biographical essays, Arthur wrote a sympathetic but critical study of Edmond Warre, Head Master of Eton from 1884 to 1905 and Provost from 1909 to 1918. As one of his subordinates, however, Arthur fretted and fumed under his rule (as he would have done, very probably, under any headmaster). He rather grudgingly admired and respected Warre's undoubted *auctoritas*, but at the same time was quite unable to account for the sway which he commanded. His deficiencies were only too evident. 'His eloquence is nil, his arguments unsound, his knowledge limited, his prejudices extreme', Arthur wrote in July 1899, 'but yet he is personally impressive in a high degree.' And again, three years later: 'The more one thinks of him the more his *greatness* emerges. I mean that he is undoubtedly a great man; and when I am in his presence I am entirely dominated by him – but he is no teacher, not learned, no speaker, no preacher. I disagree with him on all educational subjects, and yet I recognise and admire his force.'

It was therefore with some trepidation that Arthur faced the prospect of staying with Warre at his country home, Baron's Down in Somerset, for a week-end in January 1903 (not actually the first time he had been there). Arthur had just published *The Schoolmaster*, a collection of essays attacking several of Warre's most cherished ideals (or extreme

97

prejudices, whichever way one cared to regard them); most notably, the predominantly classical curriculum at Eton. This labelled Arthur as something of an educational reformer, and he had become the spokesman – although a classical tutor himself – of the group of disaffected non-classicists on the Eton staff, who were attempting to challenge the monopoly of the classical staff within the Tutorial system, which accorded them a higher prestige within the School.

So off Arthur went to Baron's Down. The portrait of Warre in his domestic setting – very much 'Farmer Warre', an aspect which the boys rarely saw – is not an unkindly one; but it is emphatically unreverential, and has that graphic quality, veering towards caricature, which is typical of Arthur's finest descriptive passages.

Changed at Taunton; I liked the great flat by Bristol as usual. Then we glided into the Somersetshire valleys. It had been raining and there was a good deal of water about in the fields. I liked the gentle undulations, the red soil of the fields, the velvety meadows, the soft brown of leafless trees, the pale light of the winter evenings on the wet roads. There was a delightful vignette of four horses drawing logs at Morebath; and I liked the little Somersetshire villages on the ridges of climbing slopes, with the soft green valleys going off into the hills. I was cheerful but a little weary.

At Dulverton I was greeted by a loud cry, and Philip Williams, as a country squire, with gun in case and holding a bunch of pheasants, came towards me. I felt rather overpowered by his geniality. A young nice groom drove me up through Dulverton. If I had been superstitious, I had food for omens: an interminable train of rooks, hundreds and hundreds, the black-coated gentry, came floating from Baron's Down over my head and lit in the high dusky wood to the left. High up on the right I saw Pixton in its clumps. We went through Dulverton to get letters; a nice irregular little town; and then after a very steep pitch came into the Barlinch valley; and I soon saw Baron's Down perched white and flat-faced at the top corner of the great steep brown wood. We went very slowly up the drive among the newly cut rhododendrons, the day falling. . . .

(The house) has a squat white front with a pillared portico – does not look nearly so large as it is. It has large square high rooms, which would be very difficult to decorate and which would never look well. On each side of the door is a large kind of parlour – the drawing-room cheaply furnished with fair comfort; the morning-room rather bare and messy. Out of the hall opens a little gun room and the stairs go up. To the left, down two steps is the dining-room; opening out of that, the smoking-room, a small muggy room; and then out of that, the study with a bow-window.

The study is ugly with the peculiar kind of ugliness which Warre communicates to the rooms he lives in – the paper hideous; the fireplace of a sort of 'Maple-Suite' type. There are huge chairs; one called by Warre 'Great Snorum'. The whole house seems to me to have been lately done up. There are some nice old portraits and funny little small landscapes in big frames; also a lot of old deers' heads, with delightful names of woods – 'Found Haddon and killed at Dawes-ham Wood Oct. 20, 1821' – dating from the time when the hounds were kept here.

There were some shooters going off when I arrived. Warre was visible in the brightly lighted tea-room, bustling about, big and rosy. He came out at the sound of wheels, and greeted me very warmly, shook me often by the hand, thanked me for coming. I was soon established at a large table spread with tea, Devonshire cream, toast etc. (I had had tea at Taunton). Mrs Warre was there; very kindly, nodding a good deal with a vacant eye, addressing me some mild and rather unintelligible remarks; also Joan, rosy and plump, Henry looking well, but a good deal older (just promoted to the Staff) and a mild gentleman, with red woollen slippers, reading gently in the drawing-room, introduced as General Clarke. He called Warre 'Edmond' and was himself called Charlie. I found out afterwards that he was Sir Charles Mansfield Clarke,

Bt., G.C.B., Quartermaster-General, from a leather official letter-bag he had. He is just appointed Commander-in-Chief at Malta. He was a King's Scholar it seems – rather an orageux youth, but charming – Luxmoore's contemporary. He inherited the baronetcy from his grandfather, a surgeon. He seemed a mild and well-meaning man, easy-going and pleasant, but without much to say for himself.

Warre carried me off to his study, and said he was sorry to bring me so far at much inconvenience to myself, but he was simply bursting to talk about the Tutorial Question. I told him my view about defining the authority of the Classical Tutor as *sub*-ordinate; but he objected to this. I also enlightened him as to various practices that had been initiated, and also about the threats of boycotting etc. which come from the irreconcilables. He was very angry at this and talked about dismissing them etc. very violently. It is useless to talk like this: they could appeal to the Governing Body, and Warre would have no case. He gave me a little book – extracts from Jowett [Master of Balliol] – and finally took me up to my room – a large square room, very draughty, over the morning-room, where I have slept before.

We had a moderately lively dinner – but the tendency is to talk a good deal about very local events – the sheep, the dogs, the farm etc. Joan confided to me she was very sleepy – had been dancing two nights running. She described the Williams' country-house – without a picture of any kind on the walls. We had prayers in the morning-room, read incredibly fast by Warre. Then we smoked first in the drawing-room, and then adjourned to the study, Warre in a brown smoking-cap with a rug, plunged in Great Snorum, in a rubicund kind of muse; his spectacles off and his eyes closed and dreamy. The talk not interesting. Warre rumbled off to bed, and I soon after.

I slept well. In the morning the world was white, the view of the valley, the fields white and the woods dusted with snow, very beautiful. Innumerable bells tinkled. Warre descending, whistled and cried 'Bears, bears, Joan-poan!' just as he did when I was here last, twelve years ago(?). I descending found Warre and the General soberly at breakfast. It seems that Warre has to say 'Very good fish – help yourself' to *everyone*. But it was pleasant to see Warre's contented happiness, he was rosy and beaming with pleasure, and talked really laughable nonsense. The General and Felix [Warre] were to drive off at 12.0 to catch a train at Tiverton. They had only shot twelve pheasants the day before. Till then I dawdled about in mild depression; read educational reports and Jowett in Warre's study. At 12.0 they went off, Sir Charles in fur-coat, very neat and precise, like a gallant knight; Felix, bluff, big and cheerful. He was a little boy not at school when I was here last (I remember then a funny scene of Edmond *junior* wandering round the table to say goodnight, full of sleep and heavy-eyed, offering to kiss me and then being overcome with childish shame).

Then we had a service read by the household – too snowy to go to Church – in the morning-room, with the sun streaming in. I never heard a service read faster – Warre in a short black coat and black tie, huge spatted feet, with his glasses off, holding a book to his face, and screening himself from the bright sun with a huge soft hand. Then lunch. Then we walked very slowly (I in a pair of Warre's gaiters, which fitted me exactly – another omen!) about his terraces, sloped gardens, greenhouses, policies. The cold melting snow very deep was unpleasant. Then, with Henry, we went all round the farm across frozen fields deep with snow. Saw the brown bleak sides of Dunkery to the North. To the East, the brown back of Haddon. We loitered fearfully, Warre (he is 66) going very slow and dressed like a sort of farmer. Henry left us and we went back to the gardens again. Here he became autobiographical and consequently interesting. He talked of leaving Baron's Down. He had had it for twenty-one years; it cost him £1000 a year; but the boys were less and less able to come for holidays, and he thought of buying a small place of his own. He said suddenly, with the strange lapse into semi-emotional metaphysics that characterises him, that he had learnt that one 'possessed' nothing in the world. Then he began to talk of his health – much improved – and his wish to stay at Eton and reform the system. 'I feel I have a work to do.' He turned on me suddenly,

'Speaking frankly – do the masters desire me to go? – Are they contented and happy?' He looked mildly at me. Que dire? I couldn't tell him in his own garden that we wanted him to go – so I murmured feebly and lost my chance.

After tea he unfolded to me his scheme, with red and blue pencils, drawn very clumsily on blotting paper. It was no scheme at all. He said 'We mustn't have a modern school. We must say boldly that we give a classical education. We must have a good general Trunk scheme up to the top of Lower Division and specialise later. We must keep Greek. I know you won't agree with me.' And then he went on about Curzon liking the Odyssey – he really only quotes it in his letter to please Warre – and the Dean liking to construe the Greek Testament. In fact his scheme is to keep the present system intact and specialise a little more – and call it a reform. He really is hopeless, I fear.

Then we discussed the Tutorial system. He wouldn't have any such word as *sub*ordinate, but suggested *omitting* the objectionable paragraph. This is, I think, a wise and sensible compromise. He again expressed gratitude to me for coming. He spoke of his successor – 'I don't know who it is to be, except perhaps Rawlins[1]', he said.

We dined quietly – drank Consumo – I had a little talk to Henry about his feelings in action. He took a gloomy view of [General Sir Redvers] Buller – described the awful sight of seeing Long's guns lost before their eyes – and his last sight of Freddy Roberts, shot through stomach and limbs broken – quite conscious.[2] Roberts said: 'My God, Warre, don't get within reach of the Boer bullets.' Then I went in to Warre. He was grumpy. His mood had altered, and he sate looking old and crumpled in his chair, smoking a cigar. He said that the *Schoolmaster* had done harm – embarrassed the

---

[1] F.H.Rawlins, who in the final contest in 1905 (from which A.C.B. withdrew) was adjudged to be the runner-up to Edward Lyttelton.

[2] The reference is to the disaster at Colenso on 15 December 1899 when Buller in marching to relieve White at Ladysmith was outfought by Louis Botha and lost ten guns and eleven hundred men. Frederick Roberts (Lord Roberts' only son) was killed in attempting to recover the guns.

6 The Pines, Putney Hill, the home of Swinburne and Watts-Dunton, in
1895. From a drawing by Herbert Railton
'*I was standing in a very common suburban street, with omnibuses and cabs,
and two rows of semi-detached houses going up the gentle acclivity of the hill.
I suddenly saw I was standing opposite the house, a perfectly commonplace
bow-windowed yellow-brick house, with a few shrubs in the tiny garden.*'
(p. 106)

7 Stanway, Gloucestershire. Engraving by F. L. Griggs, 1904
'I never saw such a place. A long gabled front with great mullioned windows, with a huge hall oriel. The door severely classical. All so simple and so exquisitely beautiful.' (p. 116)

defenders of Public School education; given a handle to blasphemers. 'They have quoted it, warped the statements – very unfairly – but still they have your authority.' Then when I pleaded for more leisure, he said: 'I am not in favour of that. You use it well; but others would not. They would only play and amuse themselves more. They wouldn't read.'

I slept ill and dreamed much. Woke early. Breakfasted well, and the carriage came round. It had frozen hard and the roads were slippery. We drove fast thro' the frosty air. Warre had insisted on *giving* me a pair of gaiters, like Elijah. He and Henry saw me off, gave me pheasants. Warre took a very affectionate farewell and stood waving his hand. He was dressed in brown, with gaiters, like an old squire. He went back to his sermon, which he showed me and which did not promise well.

I had a comfortable journey in a warm corridor train and read Zola's *Assommoir*. I became entirely absorbed. He relentlessly lays bare the descent through drink of a good man and woman into an abyss of profligacy and wretchedness. He draws no moral, upholds no hope – a ghastly book. The mistake made is treating such a downfall as typical, whereas I expect it is wholly abnormal. I finished it as we rolled through Southall, having seen and heard nothing, and coming up like a diver out of a pool. I came to the Grosvenor Club, where I write this. I gather from the conversation that we are to be ejected from these premises, which have been a happy little oasis to me for a good many years. I am sorry for this, but I suppose we must consent to be pilgrims!

While I sate and read in the library I was aware of a voice, and the high white forehead, beaky nose and receding chin of Churchill[3] came in sight, who gave me a message from Henry James that he was feeling neglected. I then listened, affecting to read, while a glorious young man, of rather loose life, I gathered, talked to the Bright Particular Bore of the Grosvenor – *the Major* – the large purple-faced man with the gruff voice – and read aloud to

---

[3] E. L. Churchill, a much younger Eton colleague and great defender of the classical curriculum.

him a letter from America from a mutual friend, interspersed with many chuckles and oaths. 'Well, Major, so you'd like to hear what Randall says. Damn it, he *is* a good chap and no mistake. Here we are: "Dear old bloke" – ha, ha, damn it – "here I am sitting down to write to you just after having partaken of my Christmas cheer – no roast beef and plum duff here, my boy, – no, no, we do things better – a pair of canvassed back ducks" – and so he goes on, – h'm, h'm – *what* a chap he is, damn it – a damnation sight better than most of the chaps here. "We had *four* bottles of Pommey" – how does that strike you, Major? – *four* bottles – hey? Ha, ha – what an old guzzle he is. Then there's a P.S. about you, Major: "I am surprised that the Major still goes hanging round Winifred Thornton: he ought to know better at *his* age." Ha, ha! How does *that* strike you, Major – Pamplin has pretty well taken the measure of the Major, I think, damn it all – *very* good – Ought to know better, eh? How does *that* strike you, Major?' – and so on – the Major inaudible, punctuating it with apoplectic rumblings.

[Volume 22, pp.76–96]

VIII

$\diamond$

He meets Algernon Swinburne at his house in Putney

As Arthur became increasingly fidgety at Eton, deploring the drudgery of so much of the working-day, pining for the freedom to work at leisure, he came more and more to envy the relative independence of his literary friends, especially Henry James and Edmund Gosse. If only he could find the right subject, the right opening – he resolved – he would abandon Eton with profound relief and settle himself for a literary career. He therefore accepted with alacrity the invitation to write a study of D.G.Rossetti for the *English Men of Letters* series, a venture which was to lead to other commissions from the same source – studies of Edward Fitzgerald, William Morris and Walter Pater.

To understand Rossetti he had to be able to gain entry into the strange, and no longer fashionable, world of Pre-Raphaelitism; and his obvious starting-point was to arrange a meeting with Algernon Swinburne, who lived in eccentric seclusion with his companion, the pretentious and self-important Theodore Watts-Dunton, in a faded and drab-looking villa in Putney.

The account of this visit on 4 April 1903 in Arthur's diary is well worth reproducing in full. It is, for instance, a perfect illustration of the diarist's 'microscopic eye', missing nothing, noting every gesture, every inflection, every aside, every little detail and oddity about the house and garden, with a sort of relish of anticipation at the prospect of committing the whole to paper at the earliest opportunity. It also reveals something of particular significance in Arthur Benson's temperament and character. He would have liked to have been part of an acknowledged literary circle; but the fascination of the circle was much more his delight in *observing* it from the wings, so that he could revel in its absurdities, than any satisfaction that he might derive from the sense of being accepted within the circle itself. As with other groups and circles of Edwardian England to which Arthur might have expected naturally to belong, so too with this. He liked to be *of* it (so that he could observe and chronicle its doing in his diary), but he had not the least desire to be *in* it.

I left my house on a bicycle about 12.0. and rushed up town after an unsatisfactory morning of odds and ends. I had been received by Mr Watts-Dunton with a great amount of epistolary ceremony, many courteous letters arranging my visit, written by a secretary. The day was dark and gloomy. I got to Putney about 1.15 and walked into the street; I asked my way to the house expecting it to stand high up. I was standing in a very common suburban street, with omnibuses and cabs, and two rows of semi-detached houses going up the gentle acclivity of the hill. I suddenly saw I was standing opposite the house, a perfectly commonplace bow-windowed yellow-brick house, with a few shrubs in the tiny garden. I went up to the door, and was at once taken in by a maid. The house was redolent of cooking, dark, not very clean-looking, but comfortable enough – the walls crowded everywhere with pictures, mostly Rossetti's designs in pen and ink or chalk. I was taken into a dining-room on the right looking out at the back. To the left the tall backs of yellow-brick houses; the gardens full of orchard trees in bloom. A little garden lay beneath with a small yew hedge and a statue of a nymph, rather smoke-stained, some tall elms in the background.

Meets Algernon Swinburne at Putney

Mr Watts-Dunton came out and greeted me with great cordiality. He seemed surprised at my size, as I was similarly surprised at his – and had not remembered he was so small. He was oddly dressed in waistcoat and trousers of some greenish cloth and with a large heavy blue frock-coat, too big for him with long cuffs. He was rather bald, with his hair grown rather thick and long and a huge moustache which concealed a small chin. He had lost his teeth since I saw him and looked an old man, though healthily bronzed and with firm small hands. After a compliment or two he took me upstairs. There lay a pair of elastic-sided boots outside a door, the passage thickly carpeted and pictures everywhere. He went quickly in, the room being over the dining-room.

There stood before me a little pale, rather don-like man, quite bald, with a huge head and domelike forehead, a ragged red beard in odd whisks, a small aquiline red nose. He looked supremely shy but received me with a distinguished courtesy, drumming on the ground with his foot and uttering strange little whistling noises. He seemed very deaf. The room was crammed with books; bookcases all about – a great sofa entirely filled with stacked books – books on the table. He bowed me to a chair, 'Will you sit?' On the fender was a pair of brown socks. W.D. said to me 'he has just come in from one of his long walks', took up the socks and put them behind a coal scuttle. 'Stay!' said Swinburne, and took them out carefully holding them in his hand, 'they are drying.' W.D. murmured something to me about his fearing they would get scorched, and we sate down. Swinburne sate down concealing his feet behind a chair and proceeded with strange motions to put the socks on out of sight. 'He seems to be changing them' said W.D. Swinburne said nothing but continued to whistle and drum.

Then he rose and bowed me down to lunch, throwing the window open. We went down and solemnly seated ourselves, W.D. at the head, back to light; Swinburne opposite to me. We had soup, chickens, many sweets, plovers' eggs. Swinburne had a bottle of beer which he drank. He was rather tremulous with his hands and clumsy. At first he said nothing, but gazed at intervals out of the window with a mild blue eye, and a happy sort of look.

Watts-D. and I talked gravely, W.D. mumbling his food with difficulty. When he thought that Swinburne was sufficiently refreshed he drew him gracefully into the conversation. I *could* not make Swinburne hear, but W.D. did so without difficulty. He began to talk about Hawthorne; he said that *The Scarlet Letter* was a great book, but that any book *must* be a bathos after such a first chapter. 'I want more catastrophe for my money.' He smiled at me. Then he went on to speak of *The House with Seven Gables*, and then of certain dramas which were names to me – *Le Tourneur* etc. He waxed very enthusiastic over Elizabeth Arden(?), which he said was as great as Shakespeare, greater than Romeo and Juliet or the early plays. He said it was published in 1598(?) and that if it was *not* by Shakespeare there was the extraordinary fact of a dramatist living at the same time as Shakespeare who could create and embody a perfectly natural supreme woman.[1]

He seemed content to be silent, and I was struck with his great courtesy, esp. to W.D. This was very touching. W.D. made some criticism on Scott (Swinburne having said the *Bride of Lammermuir* was a *perfect* story) about the necessity when Scott became bookish of translating him into patois. 'Very beautiful and just' said Swinburne, looking affectionately and gratefully at W.D. 'I have never heard that before and it is just. You must put that down.' W.D. smiled and bowed. Later on W.D. attributed some opinion to Rossetti – 'Gabriel thought etc.' Swinburne smiled and said 'I have often heard you say that, but' (he turned smiling to me) 'Mr Benson, there is no truth in it. Rossetti had no opinions when I first knew him on Chatterton and many other subjects – and our friend here had merely to say a thing to him and it was absolutely adopted and fixed in the firmament.' W.D. stroked Swinburne's small pink hand which lay on the table and Swinburne gave a pleased schoolboy smile.

Lunch being over, Swinburne looked revived, and talked away merrily. He bowed me out of the room with ceremony. W.D. seemed to wish me to stay and Swinburne looked concerned, drew

---

[1] It seems likely that the play to which Swinburne was referring was *Arden of Feversham* published in 1592 and attributed by some to Shakespeare.

nearer to him and said 'Mr Benson must come and sit a little in my room' – so we went up. Swinburne began pulling down book after book and showed them to me, talking delightfully. As he became more assured he talked rhetorically. He has a full firm beautiful pronunciation, and talks like one of his books. Occasionally his voice went into a little squeak. He suddenly rose and went and drank some medicine in a corner. He had on an odd black tail-coat, a greenish waistcoat and slippers; low white collar, made-up tie – very shabby indeed. There was an odd bitter bookish scent about the room, which hung I noticed about him too.

He talked a little about Eton and Warre, saying 'he sate next me many a half and he was a good friend of mine'. Then W.D. proposed that I should go, when Swinburne said, half timidly, 'I hope there is time just to show Mr Benson one of these scenes.' – 'Well, one scene', said W.D., 'but we have a lot of business to talk. You read it to him.' He took the book I was holding – the Arden play – and read very finely and dramatically, with splendid inflections, a fine scene; his little feet kicked spasmodically under his chair and he drummed on the table. He was pleased at my pleasure; and then took up some miracle plays, and told me a long story of the Annunciation of the Nativity in it – the sheep-stealer, called Mack, who steals a sheep and puts it into the child's cradle; the shepherds come to find it and laugh; then the angel appears. 'Do you think Mr Benson will be shocked if I show him what Cain says?', he said, and showed me giggling a piece of ancient schoolboy coarseness. W.D. smiled indulgently.

Then at last W.D. took me away. Swinburne shook hands with great cordiality, and a winning shy kind of smile lighting up his pale eyes. I was haunted by a dim resemblance to William Sidgwick[2]. W.D. led me off, saying 'I like him to get a good siesta. He is such an excitable fellow. He is like a schoolboy – unfailing animal spirits, always pleased with everything; but he has to take care.' He was much amused at Swinburne asking me if I was his contemporary at Eton.

---

[2] The Revd William Sidgwick, Arthur's uncle (brother of Henry Sidgwick).

Meets Algernon Swinburne at Putney

I was somehow tremendously touched by these two old fellows living together (Swinburne must be 66 and W.D. about 72?), and paying each other these romantic compliments and displaying distinguished consideration; as though the world was young. I imagine that the secret of W.D.'s influence is that he is ready to take all the trouble off the shoulders of these eminent men; that he is very sedulous, complimentary, gentle – and that he is at the same time just enough of an egotist to require and draw out some sympathy.

He is certainly a *great* egotist, and not, in any technical sense, a gentleman. He drops his h's; he pronounces 'prowl' *'proal'*, 'cloud' *'clowd'*, 'round' *'roaned'* etc. He leads the talk back and back to himself. I will give some instances of this first. He kept on saying that he didn't say and didn't do this or that. 'Good God, the world's a great whispering gallery' and he seemed to have quite a disproportionate sense of the place he occupied in the world's eye. Here is this kind old gentleman, living in the glow of the embers of two great literary friendships, in a comfortable frowsy kind of house at Putney, and thinking that he is a kind of pivot on which the world turns. But then he has excuses. His absurd book (*Aylwin*) flies into a twentieth edition. Rossetti tells him that the figure of 'Rosabell' in *The Coming of Love* is the most living breathing vital thing since Shakespeare. *I* should believe myself a great and inspired poet on much less. And after all, what harm does it do? To take oneself seriously is the great happiness of life.

W.D. kept – all through our long talk (we sate from 2.30 to 5.0) – reverting to himself: how *he* was the only man not dominated by Rossetti; how dogs wouldn't bite him; how as a boy at school, *he* dominated all the school, so that no boy ever got a hamper without bringing it to W.D. for him to choose what he liked best (he called it a very big fashionable private school) and would have carried him about all day on their shoulders if he had desired it; and how no edict of the masters would have availed, if he had given contrary orders.

He sighed heavily at one time and said that he had himself not done what he ought to have done in literature. At this I poured in a good deal of rather rancid oil and ginger-wine. He smiled indulgently and deprecatingly, and then said that the charge of Rossetti had been very anxious – the strategems to reduce chloral, the dancing attendance on his whims. But he said: 'In his friendship and the friendship of Swinburne I find my consolation.' This I did not think sincerely said.

'Swinburne', he said several times over, 'is a mere boy still – and must be treated like one – a simple schoolboy, full of hasty impulses and generous thought – like April showers.' He added 'his mental power grows stronger every year – everybody's does – he is now a pure and simple improvisatore.'

W.D. sipped a little whisky and water and smoked a cigarette. He sometimes reclined in an armchair; sometimes came and sate near me. I sate in a great carved chair of Rossetti's (very fine – Indian) facing the light. There were fine pictures everywhere: a *most* interesting one of Rossetti reading poetry to Watts-Dunton in the Green Room at 16 Cheyne Walk, by Dunn. He gave me a reproduction of this; a Shakespeare in a heavy frame; beautiful witches of Rossetti, in crayons, pale red, peeping out of great gold frames. Outside [were] the white orchard blooms and trees – and I arranged myself so that I could see no house-backs, and we might have been at Kelmscott.

I now transcribe as accurately as I can what he told me about Rossetti, in answer to many questions.

Rossetti was *not* a hard worker. He had *no* permanent quarrel with Morris. Mackail's book, he said, was a mere *joke*. Morris had a peculiar dislike to Mackail, and it was as Burne Jones's friend that Mackail did it. It was not what Rossetti *did* that impressed you. It was what he *was*. His work was nothing. It came streaming out irrepressibly as heat from radium. He had an extraordinary effect on everyone (except W.D.) and dominated them. 'Look at Swinburne's poetry. Swinburne has no animal nature at all – a mere bookman and a schoolboy. *The feminine and sensuous element in Swinburne's poetry was entirely under Rossetti's influence.*'

Mystical passion, he said, was the root idea of Rossetti's life. 'That was his life – yes, that was his life', he said very gravely and impressively. He was *very* susceptible to female charm; and women fell wildly in love with him. W.D. had refused to introduce a lady-friend of his to Rossetti. She kept on asking why. 'Because you are a married woman – a beautiful woman – and if he falls in love with you, I won't answer for the consequences.' He had no *conscience* in the matter, though superstitious and in other ways much troubled by conscience. The odd Holman Hunt quarrel was this: Holman Hunt had a young model, Annie Miller, a simple pretty girl, to whom he was engaged. When he went out to the East, he committed her to Rossetti's charge. 'Good God', said W.D., 'the folly of committing such a girl to so susceptible and so dominant a man!' However, Rossetti did *not* fall in love with her (and when W.D. once questioned him as to whether he had in any way played Holman Hunt false about it, he answered very angrily that he would not have behaved so to H.H., and moreover that he had never any temptation to act otherwise). But he saw a great deal of the girl; took her about to restaurants and music-halls. Holman Hunt heard of all this, when he came back; was very angry, broke off with the girl and married someone else and broke with Rossetti – 'very unfairly', said Watt-Dunton.

Rossetti's engagement to Miss Siddal was too long protracted (ten years – I found I knew all the dates better than W.D.). She was *sewing* in a back shop when Deverell saw her. She was indescribably lovely, but not very clever (tho' Swinburne thought so), but about 55? Rossetti fell in love with Mrs Morris, then a girl, daughter of an Oxford tradesman (W.D. would not mention her name, but said 'a dear friend of mine' represented 'in that picture behind you' – afterwards saying 'that is Mrs Morris'). But Morris was also in love; and Rossetti, between friendship to Morris and loyalty to Miss Siddal, gave her up. Miss Siddal was fiercely in love with Rossetti. Rossetti was good and kind to her, but neglected her a good deal. Mrs Rossetti was very unhappy.

He went on to talk of his humour – not *delicate*, but *fancy in rapid evolution*. He was never tolerant of any subject he did not feel interested in and used to put it indignantly or contemptuously away. He would talk of art, poetry, people, life, character; loathed politics.

He did not re-touch his poems much; but was a great corrector *in print*. Like Tennyson, he did not seem to realise what a poem was, until he saw it in print.

These really interesting things were sandwiched in with a lot of rot – about a girls' school at New York and a girl of Caribbean origin etc. He said to me very gravely, 'I shall *not* write the life of Gabriel. I cannot. I knew him *too well*. He told me too much about himself – day after day, year after year.'

I had intended to go earlier but we talked on. Occasionally he went to his secretaries. Before I went, we had some tea; and then he brought in two little framed pictures (Rossetti in Green Room and Kelmscott), prepared for his illustrated *Aylwin* – and the illustrated edition of *Aylwin* itself, and gave them to me, with many expressions of kindness and cordial offers of help. '*Come* and see me', he said. 'Don't write. My correspondence is a simple curse. I have thirty letters a post' (I wonder what about?).

He wrote my name in the book. He talked a good deal about Lord de Tabley, or rather a good deal of the influence he had over de Tabley! I can't understand this enigma – how this egotistical, ill-bred, little man can have established such relations with Rossetti and Swinburne. There must be something fine about him, and his extraordinary kindness is perhaps the reason. But his talk, his personal habits (dripping moustache etc) and his egotism would grate on me at every hour of the day. And yet 'he is a hero of friendship' said Rossetti.

I went out with my precious parcel; back by train in driving rain to Windsor.

[Volume 27. pp.44–68]

IX

◇

He explores the countryside round Broadway

In the summer of 1903 Arthur Benson received an invitation, indirectly from the King, to edit – with Lord Esher – the letters of Queen Victoria. He had no doubts about accepting. This was the opportunity he had been waiting for to break loose from Eton; and by the end of the year he found himself freed from the 'drudgery' of schoolmastering – a free-lance at last. He moved to the Old Granary at Cambridge. He set to work on the royal archives at Windsor in February 1904, staying with A.C. Ainger at Eton during the period that he was needed at the Castle. This editorial work certainly did not satisfy even his immediate literary ambitions. His book on Rossetti had just been published; he was working on a further study, in the same series, on Edward FitzGerald. But what he chiefly longed to produce was a more reflective and personal book – a series of discursive essays, perhaps – if only he could find the right theme, the proper setting, the appropriate genre.

The Cotswolds holiday, in April 1904, proved to be something of a landmark in Arthur's life. It was one of the most successful and happiest breaks he had ever taken, choosing as his companion his closest Eton friend and colleague, Herbert Tatham. It was his first visit to the Cotswolds; and – as is clear from his descriptions – he found it the ideal terrain for the sort of rides and walks he liked best, with so much to delight the eye, in the natural scenery, the houses, the churches (and the monuments, too), that he felt inspired as never before in trying to understand the inexplicable mystery of the nature of beauty itself. 'Beauty, beauty, what is it? Is it only a trick of old stone and lichens and sunlight? ... One can't explain it, but it is there!' So Broadway came to provide for Arthur the setting for *The Upton Letters* (the name itself came from a quick perusal of a map of the area) and supplied the mood, the atmosphere, the inspiration: a book of letters from a schoolmaster, holidaying in the Cotswolds, reflecting on people, ideas, books, education, beauty itself. Many other such books were to come from Arthur's pen in the future, and it was from these writings that his fortune came to be made. But *The Upton Letters* stands in a class of its own for its freshness and originality; and no later experiment in the same genre was even remotely to approach it in its quality.

Warmly welcomed at the Lygon Arms, Broadway, by a nice landlord, a gentlemanly young man interested in antiquities – anxious to restore his house. He says it is full all the summer of Americans. We have got a perfectly enchanting panelled room, full of china, to sit in. Out of this opens my bedroom, about thirty feet long, with a huge white dome in the ceiling, painted with orange stars: a piano etc. Then comes a dressing-room. The room looks into the stable-yard. Tatham beyond, looking into the street. The Cromwell room has a fine stone fireplace and a plaster ceiling. He slept here before or after some battle. We had a good dinner. I was aweary and went to bed early; slept profoundly.

Sunday, April 10. I wrote many letters. At 11.30 we went off and struck up the street. I never saw such a delicious place. The houses all substantial places, mullioned, with stone tiles; full of character, gabled, and standing at different angles; ... no two alike. The inn itself has a fine front; add to this that the stone, whatever it is, weathers deliciously, orange in many places, with rich lichens. We struck right up into the hills and reached the Beacon, a modern solid tower standing 1000 feet up. A splendid view of a wide watered wooded plain, with hills standing out firmly – Malvern and the Clee hills, besides the nearer hills like Bredon. England is a sweet place!

There was a fine fresh West wind, and clouds but much sun. We wandered right along by woods, with fine southern views. At one place a great flash of the Severn, among steep hills. Came down on Stanway, where the Elchos[1] live; I was not prepared for this. We turned a corner in the village – and there stood one of the most enchanting Renaissance gate houses, with a *porte cochere*, I have ever seen (by Inigo Jones, I found). Debased in style, but so deliciously mellow. The Church close by – all a rich orange colour – the house itself just visible, and we got a view from the Churchyard.

I never saw such a place. A long gabled front with great mullioned windows, with a huge hall oriel. The door severely classical. All so simple and so exquisitely beautiful, with the wooded hill rising steeply behind. We tried to get a view of the other front, but the wall of the garden, a rich brown, with double oeil-de-boeuf windows at intervals, was too high; but the mystery made it even more poetical.

It is not only the beauty of these houses but the thought of the human associations that I love – the groups in the garden, the boy going to school, the marriage party and the funeral crossing the court with the beating bell. All these things seem to have soaked into the place, joy and sorrow alike.

We went on at last to Stanton, also a village of delightful houses, with an enchanting church, late perpendicular. Service was going on and we heard them sing the Easter Hymn from the porch, rather drowsily and very flat. But Stanton manor! It looks over with its sober gables and plain mullions into the churchyard – an

---

[1] Of the family of the Earl of Wemyss and March. A.C.B. knew the Elchos through his contacts with 'the Souls', especially George Wyndham, Mrs Grenfell (Lady Desborough) and the Grenfell boys at Eton.

almost perfect place – and the front, recessed, with two little square gabled turrets, is as good as the back. Commonsense, and natural taste, and material and weather all have gone to the making of such a beautiful place. Then we had rather a dull tramp by pleasant roads, the hills on our right running steeply up well-wooded but with pleasant combes and tumbled pasture fields. It is delicious country because it has real hill and real plain – and these incomparable houses.

Let me remember one or two touches of *colour* – the yellow flowering shrub (Japanese, I think – it grows by the pavilion at Eton) peeping over the wall of Stanton manor; and a fresh green columbine rooting itself in the stones of a little brown-stained bridge. These were like musical phrases.

We entered Broadway by the lower end, by what was once a farm, but which some rich and delicate-minded person has made into a charming house, using the barn as a great hall. The big loop-holed barns everywhere are perfect.

We had been out about five hours – no fatigue; and one of the most delightful walks I have had for years. Now we sit in the panelled parlour, with a clock ticking and the street outside very silent. On the mantelpiece are copper and pewter vessels, very pleasant to look at. We dined and read. I went to bed and slept like a top, but woke at 3.0., and heard a shrill clock tell the hour, followed by a clock that seems to thump out the strokes. I lay awake, very cheerfully, till 5.0., when I drew aside the blind and found the divine morning coming in over the stable yard. Cocks crew faintly and horses rattled and munched in the stables. Then I slept again.

Monday, April 11. Wrote a few letters; but went off at 10.20 to Evesham – a dull road; crossed a bridge and a river. Evesham lies in a loop. I felt a sudden and violent faintness on rushing up the hill into the town, but it did not return. Just caught a train and got to Ashchurch, a place with many lines crossing each other. I never saw a more junctional place. Rode to Tewkesbury, a dull road, and entered by low slummy streets, but were soon in the better part of the town.

Tewkesbury is a pleasing place – nice comfortable red-brick houses mixed with old timbered leaning fronts. It was a cool day, but with plenty of sun. We were soon at the Abbey and went through the trim graveyard. I don't mean to describe antiquities, but it is a grand place; the huge barrel-like pillars, the low vaulting; all opulent and well kept; a rich rector, Verburgh, whom I knew and whose boys were down for my house. The chapels and chantries are delicious, and there are many moving historical things. The Duke of Clarence (drowned in the butt of malmsey) lies in a vault with his duchess; Hugh Despenser, favourite of Edward II – a young man, Duke of Warwick, King of the Isle of Wight, Jersey and Guernsey who died at 21 – lies in the choir. A beautiful Early English tomb in the South East choir aisle, *most* beautiful. I wished they had made such a one at Canterbury. A huge new organ in a transept. A wasted figure in a shroud, a mouse nibbling his entrails, and worms, snails and toads creeping over him – a piece of *pure* decadence.

I feel nowadays, what I never used to feel, a great going out of the heart to all these people, who lived and loved the earth and the glory of it – who have died and gone into the darkness. I remembered them all in a little prayer before the altar, and wondered where and what they were this bright morning, with the world all so pleasantly arranged for me. I hope they are not mere rich memories, but one tends to exaggerate the part that *men* play and have played in the world of God. We walked hither and thither ... Then we bicycled on to Deerhurst. Saw the odd oblong tower over the fields – a dull country just here – we got up to it and into a farmyard. Such a picturesque place. The farm is the old Refectory and Prior's Lodging and joins the Church. Where the apse was is a cartshed and byre, above which the Church rises steeply. An old farmer came and welcomed us and told us we were trespassing in a breath. Then we got the key and saw the quaint Church – such a place. It is *the oldest* building in England which is still put to its original use. It was an Abbey in 804!! Then a kind of

8 A photograph by
Sir Benjamin
Stone of the Lygon
Arms, Broadway,
1904
*'Warmly welcomed
at the Lygon Arms,
Broadway, by a
nice landlord, a
gentlemanly young
man interested in
antiquities – anxious
to restore his
house.'* (p. 115)

9 Arthur Balfour's house, Whittingehame, East Lothian
   'The whole thing surprised me by its opulence and its magnificence. It is a very big, imposing house of grey stone; and the whole place trim, groomed, splendidly kept, with an air of great wealth lavishly used.' (p. 146)

10 The Garden at Whittingehame
   'Then we saw the little red tower, with Douglas arms, that is the original fortress of the mansion.' (p. 150)

fortress, the Abbot sleeping in the tower, which is all Saxon and herring-bone work. . . .

We sate by a yew tree in the churchyard and lunched. The spell of the place was very strong on me. It lies there in the quiet fields, so old and holy, and all mellowed and softened down into such quiet fragrance and repose, the history all gone and nothing left but a kind of peaceful association.

Then we had to go on; and we went down by the chapel – and lo and behold, we were on the banks of the great silent speeding Severn, running by red banks 'too full for sound and foam'. We made our way back to Tewkesbury by rich watermeadows, the river running blue between its high banks. Such a sweet place, all hemmed in with a long bank of trees. It was this, of course, that determined the place of the old monastery, which once owned 40,000 acres. The Dissolution is a fearful and inexplicable tragedy – the sudden smashing up of all these peaceful wealthy houses; but I suppose that they must have been feared and dreaded.

We were at Tewkesbury by 3.30. We explored a little; crossed Avon and went to a bridge over Severn, by a great red cliff. Such a fine scene, the rich watermeadows, the town with factories spouting smoke and the quiet Abbey at the end of it. Over the ridge appeared the blue Malvern hills, with their noble outline.

Tatham met a boy of his in the town; and we saw a King's Scholar called Laffan, walking along with two small boys arm-in-arm with him. He saluted gravely. I forget I am no longer a master! Then comes a little soft pang of regret – but I would not go back if I could. We rode very briskly back by pleasant roads under the hills . . . and we were at Broadway by 5.0. Had tea; pleasantly tired, but not exhausted. Dined 7.30. Read Victor Hugo's *Travailleurs de la Mer*, and thought how W.J.[2] used to love it, and used to quote Lilliatt buying the wild sea-birds from the boys and letting them go again. V.H. is too ludicrous in his love for *detailed* facts which he

---

[2] W. Johnson Cory, the Eton master who was in many ways A.C.B.'s mentor, although they never met. Arthur's love for Cory came largely from reading his letters and journals.

gets all wrong. But the beautiful deep-reaching feeling is like a well of hill-water.

This has been a really perfect day – such variety of sight and sound. We have covered so much ground and seen such different things, each with a characteristic charm. The thought of Deerhurst, the ancient church by the Severn, with the farm – like an old man asleep and dozing in his chair – all the history of it gone; and yet there, is a parable which I shall not easily forget. We dined well; but I slept ill.

Tuesday, April 12. A beautiful bright day, with a strong East wind and hazy. We wrote letters. . . . While I sate writing, two men carried a coffin with brass fittings cheerfully down the street; then a pack of hounds came through. We started at 11.30 and sped very pleasantly across to Elmley Castle.

The great mass of Bredon loomed in the haze. We sate for a few minutes on the crest of a little hill, and explored a tiny copse or dingle, where there had once been a cottage and an orchard; now a little field, ringed round with thickets, and simply carpeted with violets, ranging from large purple ones to nearly white. This delicious thicket reached a long way among the hills; but we had no time to explore. We were soon at Elmley Castle – a pleasant little village; at the head of it a church and a big house and a huge park reaching right up the hill. Such a very beautiful quiet seemly place. A lake behind the Church. Inside it was fresh and trim. A fine Jacobean monument; and an amusing one of an Earl of Coventry. A man in a great periwig, in an alcove, as if fallen down when skating, pointing feebly at an earl's coronet with a shapely hand, attended by females and cupids.

Ran on again to Pershore; the country rather dull. Suddenly coming over a slope, the huge tower became visible below us among pear-trees. We were soon at the bridge, a fine old bridge, and a sparkling river in green fields. Wickenden[3] was curate here long ago. It is a vast poor parish, the abbey being only a chapel of

---

[3] J. F. Wickenden, a close friend of Edward White Benson.

ease. ... The place all solemn and stately, but like a big body
without a soul. I suppose that only in England are to be found these
fine churches almost unendowed and yet served by rich clergy
who willingly spend all their private means in keeping the places
beautiful. The people seem proud of their churches, but don't
attend them much. That is very English too. ...

Then on again to Worcester: the country dull and switch-
backy. At last came suburbs, and then Worcester, a smoking town
below us. We went to the station, discovered trains, and to the
Cathedral. It has been restored out of all interest by Gilbert Scott,
and decorated in horrible taste. But it is rich and splendid in a way.
I was much struck by the tomb of King John, who rests, a seemly
gilt figure, before the high altar: a noble chantry to Prince Arthur,
Henry VIII's elder brother. How different things might have been
if he had succeeded to the throne.

Saw many old and beautiful tombs of Lords and Bishops – two
dreadful modern ones of Lord Lyttelton and Lord Dudley, like
butlers in bed. Two monuments amused us much. One to Bishop
Hough (the man who was turned out of Magdalen). He sits in
lawn-sleeves on the edge of a precarious slab, his leg swinging.
Fame, a stout wench, tries her best to keep him in situ – and the
inscription may well say that 'he was placed in a dangerous
situation'. To the right a cupid, crying fat tears, displays a
medallion of Mrs Hough. There is a splendid absurd pompous
inscription, with a fine Johnsonian roll. But somehow a gallant,
courteous, worthy old fellow emerges. He held three bishoprics in
succession, and died at 98. There is also a funny monument to a
bishop, who seems cut in half by a kind of panelled box. He smiles
a quiet smile, as if amused at his situation.

We strolled in cloisters – such a sunny quiet place, all made for
work. ... Peeped in at the Deanery, once the Bishop's Palace (it
ought to be now) – such a great stately place. They are rather a
crew here; but they keep the place warm and comfortable. We
went down and saw the Severn rolling brown to the sea. The
situation is splendid. But a Worcestershire Sauce manufactory
abuts on the Deanery garden.

The countryside round Broadway

Somehow the paying of these rather idle pompous clergymen to live in these fine houses and do nothing in particular is rather irritating. I don't know what I would do, I am sure. Monopolists always get lazy and stupid. What do these well-salaried persons do, what have they to show for it all?

We strolled about, had tea at a nice bright shop, full of little tables: then I went to service, but Tatham refused. Boys in red cassocks, a lame canon. The organ was played sweetly, rather original extemporising. I sate to hear the psalms, thinking to myself (though the few persons in the nave were standing) that it didn't matter. As I went out after the psalms, a little figure came out of the seat behind me: Frank Gwatkin, my godson[4] – the one person to whom I ought to set a religious example! He was only here for a day with his mother. The psalms were poorly sung, poorly accompanied, to old fatuous chants; but I like the whole thing somehow – the warmth, the drowsy thunder of the organ, the holy smell. I don't believe in it much, but it moves me; it is a strange travesty of the kind of religion Christ came to bring; but it sets the best part of my spirit moving, for all that, and lends me wings.

We caught a train; a big express came in as we waited. One knows the kind of feeling with which, hot and tired, one looks out of a window of a train in a place like Worcester, and imagines that all the people on the platform are residents, and makes up stories about them. It was funny to see it from the other side. On the platform a little shabby rosy archdeacon talking rather cringingly to a country gent. Why not at church?

Got to Honeybourne about 5.30, and had rather a hard little ride against wind, though the places we passed on the first night – Willersley a *sweet* place – and the great hill overhanging it all gives it a great charm. We have been either bicycling or on our feet about five hours today. The only time I felt fatigue was in the Cathedral after going round with the intelligent verger. Bicycled about 30 miles. We dined very comfortably; read and smoked; it is

---

[4] Later one of A.C.B.'s undergraduate pupils at Magdalene.

now ten o'clock. One soon gets into training. I find I cannot write any original things under these conditions; but the mind swills impressions – and one does *enjoy* it all very gratefully.

Wednesday, April 13. Another perfectly delightful day. It rained in the night; but I slept like a top for ten hours and could hardly rouse myself. The sky looked heavy and unpromising. But from 11 to 5 we had six hours of perfect sunshine with fresh west winds. We went to the old Church – St Garburgh – only used in summer. Such a charming place, old and unspoilt. A painted wooden pulpit, and many Phillips monuments. A beautiful quiet tower built with no attempt to be picturesque, with a big staircase sticking out. Then up a drive to 'Kite's nest' (horrible name), formerly and decently called 'Middle-hill'. We went thro' a farmyard and beech-wood. Not a soul about. Then out on *Beacon*, with a noble view; down thro' tall gate-posts, and by a road. I talked to an old 'waller' who was resetting a wall and complimented him on his work – left him purring. Then by a great green road, Roman, I expect, along the hill, with Lord Gainsborough's big beautiful house nestling below. Then down on Chipping Campden, by woods full of primroses and anemones; and with jays, wood-peckers and other birds about.

Chipping Campden was described to me by Luxmoore [Eton colleague] as most beautiful. But the half of it was not told me! I don't honestly suppose there is any town so beautiful in England. There is a street of stone houses, every conceivable style: mullioned, gabled, devout, interspersed with pilastered Georgian houses. One with a long double oriel of exquisite work. An old pillared market-building in the centre of the street; and above it all the splendid perpendicular tower of the church. Then some Elisabethan almshouses; and in an orchard below the church two big Jacobean pavilions, with twisted chimneys and a great gateway with pepperbox towers – all disused and walled up.

We went to the Church – the vertical pinnacles streaking the sides most original; and all so beautifully weathered. Got the key at a fine old Vicarage, a stately old Vicaress giving it me and issuing directions (Mrs Carrington). The Church inside over-restored. How silly to leave black-pointed rough stonework, originally intended only for plaster and paint. A fine monument in the chancel to a worthy man, Thomas Smith. But the striking part of the Church, which was too light and fresh for beauty, was a great chapel, full of huge monuments, Jacobean, to Baptist Hickes, Lord Hickes and Viscount Campden. He was a mercer of London who was made a peer and built a great house below the Church to which the pavilions belong. The ancestor, through his daughter Juliana of the Noels, now the Gainsboroughs. The house burnt almost as soon as finished in the Civil War. Then there is another monument, with open doors, showing two shrouded figures within issuing forth: Lord Noel (who married Juliana Hickes) and his wife. Such a tender thing. He – handsome mild man; she, holding his hand and looking in his face. And then two more, with busts of pretty ladies, with curled hair, one Penelope Hickes, who 'died a mayd'. I am glad to think that these old people are still represented; tho' sorry to think that the prim Lady Victoria Buxton, whom I saw the other day, is one of their representatives. However, the stately Miss Buxton, whom I met at the Dimsdales,[5] is a better representative, rather like the Lady Penelope!

Then we went to the pavilions. They are *not* in very good taste – very rococo. But saved by age! In one, in the hole of a door-bolt, we found a robin's nest with odd squatting creatures enshrined. They stand in an orchard deep in grass, with the terraces of the old house showing. Such a sweet place, and such a text for human vanity! But the old mercer was a generous man. He built the almshouse, the market, the town-hall and everything; and his actions smell sweet and blossom in the dust.

Then we mooned about the town, bought photos and gaped at the delicious houses. Ashbee, at King's with me, has set up a Crafts Guild here – and the beauty of the place *must* soak into the workers and make them humble and sweet. Beauty, beauty! What is it? Is it only a trick of old stone and lichens and sunlight? The reviewers of

---

[5] Marcus Dimsdale, an old Eton friend, Fellow of King's College, Cambridge.

Rossetti say that R. lived 'an essentially unreal life, lost in a kind of intoxicating dream of beauty'. That only means that the reviewer does not know what beauty is. You might as well say that a farmer lived 'an essentially unreal life, lost in an intoxicating dream of agriculture'. One can't explain it, but it is there! I shall remember this sweet place as long as I live. It is not only the place; but it lies, like a lark's next, among soft green hills and woods, living its own quiet and grave life.

We struck up and over the hill and found ourselves in a splendid sandy cirque of grass, with a huge view outspread of rich watered plains, right up to Shropshire. Then down by a farm, and found a courteous old man digging a drain, like a man bursting from the grave in a resurrection. He talked slowly and genially. We asked if there was much *game*. He said: 'No – there were too many foxes; but since the new Lord Harrowby came he thought there were fewer' (he chuckled) 'most of them have had a dose of lead pills.' He directed us to Saintbury – 'past the coppice and follow a dirty lane'.

We went on – another sweet village perched on the hill-side. Saw a hen frightened by the wind banging a door close to her as tho' to frighten her. ... Then over meadows to Willersey; again these beautiful houses; at present only artists seem to have got hold of them. The sky over-clouded as we went, and the rain began to spurt, as we drew near home; just in time; and so we had another golden day. Found a lot of letters on books; and my miserable tongue began to hurt again! But nothing can take such a day away.

Thursday, April 14. Slept profoundly, but with many dreams, one *most* vivid. I was sitting in my room at *Eton*, when Sir Lewis Dibdin[6] was shown in. He said that he had been talking to the Archbishop and the Lord Chancellor and it was decided to offer me the Mastership of the Rolls – £7000 a year. I said that I had absolutely *no* legal knowledge; to which he replied that he had

---

[6] Dean of the Court of Arches, a great friend of Arthur's father.

very little to do himself and that he would gladly write my judgments for me – it was only a question of delivering a few written judgments; in fact, he said, he would be at leisure generally to sit in Court with me. He added, with tears in his eyes, that he had a great respect and affection for my father's memory and that he was glad to be able to testify it. I consented, and he told me that I must begin that morning. I was shortly robed in a black gown and full-bottomed wig and went in procession with Dibdin, feeling very great, into a vast empty hall, where we took our places on a dais at desks. There was no one else there, and it seems to me that hours passed. Dibdin sate with hands in his pockets, looking at the ceiling, whistling. I asked him what the business of the court was. He said: 'There is none today; but you must sit in case suitors appear.' Presently some American visitors were led in to see the place. I did my best to look impressive, but they laughed at me. I waited till they were gone, and then I said to Dibdin that I felt I was somehow ridiculous, and that I thought my moustache did not suit the wig; and I should shave it off. D. said 'That's right' – I then said 'I will now, with your permission, retire, as there seems to be no business, and I have important literary work on hand.' I bowed in all directions, and was stepping backwards, bowing, when Dibdin said, with a chuckle, 'Look out where you are going.' I turned round and saw that there was a huge chasm, quite a hundred feet deep; the seats being on a kind of scaffolding of posts etc. erected over it. I had to climb down by ladders and rods, to the great amusement of a large crowd below who applauded at intervals. I walked through them frowning terribly; all the while Dibdin laughed and slapped his hands, peeping over the scaffolding at the top. Then it all vanished. What is so odd is that I had no idea at the time it was funny. I thought it most serious and unpleasant, the thought of the large income and the leisure being the only solace.

It was a threatening day. We started soon after 11.0 and rode towards Stratford-on-Avon. We only stopped at Mickleton, under Meon Hill: a very attractive 18th century farm and a fine manor-house by the Church. ... Then on to Stratford, passing another fine house, being restored, in the village. The road to

The countryside round Broadway

Stratford a dull straight Roman Road, the continuation of the green drive on the hill by Campden; nice thickets occasionally, and many birds – several woodpeckers etc. We soon crossed the Stour, near Clifford Chambers and were in Warwickshire. By pleasing houses, just across the bridge, and then into Stratford.

We made straight for the Church. I had no idea it was so fine, it is a great elaborate Perpendicular Collegiate Church, with huge windows; all very richly kept. They have a great income from donations etc. There are five curates. The space under the tower between the transepts is left free of seats. The Clapton monuments are noble. There was a grand old Earl of Totnes and his countess; another to a faithful lady-in-waiting of the latter. The Earl a fine big good-humoured man. Also a Clapton tomb, rather a peevish knight. The place abounds in interesting monuments. We went to the Chancel – the fine stalls of the College still there. The Dean apparently sate at the end, on the South.

I saw the tomb and the monument of Shakespeare with very great emotion – more than I had thought possible. His wife lies by his side; they are all of them just in front of the altar ... And there he sleeps! I stood and prayed with all my might over his head, to do worthily. He is the Father and Head of all our English writing, poetry and prose; and a writer may well pray there for a double portion of that spirit. I felt the sense of the august dead very strongly. And yet both grave and monument testify to an intense desire to be like everyone else, to be rich, respectable, comfortable – not to be a mere author, but a wealthy burgher and a gentleman.

The verger obligingly brought a little ladder, and I examined the bust *very* closely. It is enormously interesting. It was whitened, by Malorie's advice, and repainted on the original colours. He wears a red kind of doublet, with a black gown over it – a large linen pall. The face is sanguine, with a very high domed forehead; curly hair on each side thin at the top; a little waxed moustache and imperial. The eyes are cheerful, the nose finely cut and shapely, the lips painfully and stiffly open, showing gum or tongue. But now that I have seen it, I have not the *faintest* doubt that it was taken from a mask taken after death. The lips have just the dry parted stiffness, the rigid smile of a dead man – only being painted vermilion, they have none of the blue and waxen pallor, as if frosted over, of death. The eyes are little sunk. But the reason why the face is unintellectual is because it is the face of a *plump* man. The cheeks rise plumply, like a plum, the chin is double. If the fat were off the face, it would be not only clever, but *very* handsome, I think.

He died at fifty-two. There is abundant evidence in the tomb and inscription that he was thought a man of exceptional ability and wit, but not more. It is strange that the grave should depend *only* on tradition, tho' the presumption amounts to a practical certainty. It is *just* opposite, on the blank wall, that that pestilent old man, Theodore Martin[7], wanted to put up his wife's bust – just opposite Shakespeare! And was only prevented by the fury of the still more pestilent Marie Corelli!

The verger, who was slightly grotesque, speaking of 'the Bard', got into his head that we were very distinguished persons, 'members of the nobility'. His curiosity increased the more we denied. He brought out an autograph book; but we declined, and wrote our names as visitors. He then followed us out, and asked if I was related to Archbishop Benson. When I admitted it, he implored me, for the Vicar's sake, to write in the State book, which I did, under the name of William Black.

Then we went to the Museum. It will be rather a fine place, I think, someday, though the theatre[8] is rather horrible, with its round end and bulging gallery. Saw many interesting things. The portraits etc. – I don't know why but I feel the bust to have been more like than the pale, egg-shaped, horrible thing, engraved for early folios, which looks a mere booby, and a dejected booby. The others mostly ridiculous. A very interesting picture of Shelley as a boy and Byron as a boy at Harrow. Also an old steel engraving of The Melancholy Jacques, which I have always loved; he sits scowling by a stream, under a mass of over-arching foliage; the

---

[7] Sir Theodore Martin, biographer of the Prince Consort.
[8] Since burnt down.

deer drink at the waterbreaks among the stones. He raises his hand and apostrophises them. Very rococo, but poetical. Some absurd pictures by Smirke – a fine one by Opie of Elizabeth Woodville saying farewell to her child. Some very funny things by Fuseli; and one by Romney(?) of Shakespeare being nursed by the *Passions* at which we laughed till we cried. The passions consist of a saucer-eyed female making faces, and two elderly men with whiskers, naked and very fat, like two partners in a firm of solicitors, making grotesque gestures.

But these pictures want more careful study; and how antiquity improves them. The stiff delineation of theatrical passion has become quaint. The Macbeth pictures are the funniest. In one two men with blue hats are talking to three Highland girls. The landscape something like the Cliveden reach on the Thames, wooded heights with castles; one of which is in flames, with the lightning that kindled it still visible across the sky. A high wind blowing; and more blue-hatted men exhibiting the most absurd and unreasonable terror of the girls. I could have stayed much longer, but we had no time.

Then to the School. Such a quaint place – a timber and plaster place, still used as a school. It was impressive to see where the stage stood for the plays in which W.S. must have taken part as a boy; and the schoolroom where he learnt a little Latin and Greek. But as if to show the spirit of the age, in the big schoolroom is nothing but a disgusting board, with the names of the School XI and Football XV painted up in gold letters. This made me very miserable. . . .

The day which had been gloomy hitherto, now began to rain heavily from great inky ragged clouds. We rushed to Shottery, and saw, rather with disgust, Ann Hathaway's cottage, smartened up and kept picturesque. A silly dressed-up girl came out with primroses and disgusted us so that we fled. Had tea in the *Silvercock* restaurant; a very superior girl, who might have been at Newnham, attending us. . . . Had a good tea; but the day being now hot and wet, and my tongue hurting, all my enthusiasm ebbed away and left me like Peter in the High Priest's Palace, instead of Moses on Sinai.

The countryside round Broadway

I am glad to have been at this great place. It is not only famous but noble in itself. It sets one wondering over the mystery: how the man can have so concealed himself from everybody; and what is still more wonderful, how glad he was to stop writing. What did he do with his mind all those peaceful prosperous years? Did he make up lines, think of characters, dream of great scenes? Did he not care to set it down? One would have thought he *must* have written. Perhaps he did not care to go back to the *older* poetry – he was never much of a rhymer – but I can't understand his contented silence. . . .

It is extraordinary how *everything* is 'Shakespeare' at Stratford. His likeness is over the Bank; his statue in the Town Hall. There are Shakespeare restaurants and stables and everything else. It was just the kind of *local* recognition that he would have liked. He only aimed at being great in Stratford. I think he was probably a good deal like Robert Browning, in his *range* of interest; but even deeper and more airy in spirit. I expect he would have been like Browning, tiresome to meet; rather pompous, proud of his position at Stratford; anxious not to speak of his books.

Friday, April 15. . . . It rained horribly and relentlessly all the morning, but seemed to clear after lunch, so out we went. We took a dull road round to Buckland and then struck up into the hills. We came to a fine old house and then the Church, beside which stands a simply enchanting gabled manor, with stone walls, orchards and a wood. Like a house in a dream. The strange thing is that I seem to have suffered and lived and been happy and sorrowful with an old house like this. I can't explain the feeling; but I seem to have loved it long ago, to have left it, returned to it, and still to love it. The Church was locked; it stands on a green terrace by the road. We went on up onto the combe. It was very hot and soft in there, like Cornwall. The sun struggled through. We climbed quickly, the house and Church lying just at the mouth of the valley; the woods full of flowers, the bushes flecked with green, birds singing sweetly. Then over the hill and round by a long level road by woods and farms making the circuit of the great Middlehill combe. .... We reached Snow's Hill – a village standing very high up, perhaps 800 feet, full again of enchanting houses – one a great mansion with a little terraced garden and farm buildings all about; a stone Georgian front. And one goes abroad to see places, with places like this unseen!

Saturday, April 16. A troubled night; I slept ill. It was hot and damp; but woke fresh. Wrote letters, and then rode about 11.30 to Evesham. It is rather a pleasing town. Found two churches and an independent tower in one churchyard. In one, some fine modern glass, and one of Kempe's insipid things. The man is flooding England with his feeble stuff – rabbit-faced people in carpets, and angels with ragged wings, The chapel where the last Abbot of Evesham lies buried was very beautiful. Evesham was one of the greatest of abbeys – nothing left but a few walls. Took train, through pear-orchards in full bloom, for Worcester and then for Malvern. Malvern is a horrid place; like Surbiton, spread out thin on the base of those grand hills. We went to the Abbey – a really magnificent church, with splendid old glass; another of these great wealthy-looking churches, warm, well-kept, well-served, comfortable. Then quickly up the hills, to the top of the Worcestershire Beacon, and then all along the range to the dip before the Hereford Beacon. This last is a grand hill, all intrenched at the top with a mighty camp, British – perhaps dating from 300 or 400 B.C. Then we left the ridge unwillingly. There are few hills so sharp and thin with such grand views both ways.

We had a house here one year – 95, I think. It was the only year I was never with them in the holidays. Papa, I remember, would not settle where to go; and finally they went off for September. .... I don't somehow think it was a success. Hugh retains a horrible recollection of it all.

Went back to Malvern by train and wandered up to see the school – very trim and smart, and utterly unattractive. I suppose that, as a schoolmaster, I ought to want to be Headmaster of a place like this – but I can trace in myself no shadow of a desire for scholastic eminence now. Little as it ever was, it all seems to have gone pop; and I think of such a life as frankly detestable. Saw Sydney's[9] comfortable house, and the new, ugly school buildings, in the sort of site that would recommend them to the ordinary parent – no grace or dignity or charm. Sate a little in a garden; then by train to Worcester; changed Foregate and again at Worcester. Got to Evesham about 5.0 and found my poor bicycle with a thorn, punctured and flat. Spent a long time mooning about, trying to find a mender. At last found a weary man in a quaint house near the Crown. We stood on the bridge, I horribly impatient, Tatham imperturbably good-tempered. The pleasant river, with neat houses all looking very agreeable, but again without charm. The chimes played 'Home, sweet home'.

At last it was done, and we rode in a cool evening to Broadway, the sun setting, and the wonderful hills lying blue against the orange glow. Got in at 7.30 and dined. I have felt rather indifferent and stupid all day, and have taken everything like cold porridge. But it is healthy, I think.

Sunday, April 17. Another *perfect* day – bright sun, a cool light wind and a few cotton-wool clouds floating high up. We started about 11.0. ... to Temple Guiting. I had wished to see this. The manor house and woods belong to Corpus, Oxford, and they want to get a tenant. The solid tower of the Church with stumpy pinnacles rose from a wood. We went down to it, and found an old clergyman and his wife walking in the Vicarage garden. The lady asked if we cared to see the Church, and got the key, a huge implement. ... She led us round the church and pointed to the Vicar's graves. 'My husband wants to lie there', she said; 'he has just been saying this morning he won't have a railing round his grave, because people won't be troubled to paint it.' He must be cheerful company! ... Then on again ... to Guiting Power, ... to Charlton Abbots ... by a winding road into the Sudeley Castle domains. ... Sudeley Castle is impressive with its long front and

---

[9] Sydney James, ex-Eton colleague, then Headmaster of Malvern.

half-ruined tower; but all along the road are gates – a dozen in all – just where you least wish to stop.

We were now in Winchcombe, a comfortable little town – a great perpendicular church, very grand and finely weathered. We met the vicar in a college cap and he showed us where to get the key. A dear old sexton with a piping voice showed us about in a leisurely way. He told us the vicar was a *doctor*. 'A doctor of divinity?', I said. 'No' (smiling) 'a doctor of literature – that ain't up to the other, is it?' He prattled on about everything, his own little house included, and gave me a very pleasant impression of a contented old age.

We saw the great stone coffin of St Kenelm – a Saxon king. We walked up the street and found a beautiful old inn, gabled, buttressed and the rest. Then we struck off home, by Toddington, and under familiar hills and by roads which we know by this time.

It was a very pleasant feeling up in the wolds, to be out in the brisk air and warm sun, miles from everything, no one knowing where one was. I have had a very gentle and pleasant feeling of content all day. This is one of the happiest days I have had for a long time. Got in and had tea; and then my restless mind began to plot out a new book! I don't know that anything will come of it. Like Cobden's daughter, I haven't very much to say. I only want to put into words some of my love for the dear earth, its hills, its flowers, its dingles – and for the houses that have here, as it were, grown up out of it! . . . The evening is closing serenely in this pleasant little street: nice family groups about house-doors; young men strolling about. Why are these rude, self-conscious, over-dressed, loud-laughing, parading young creatures so *odious* at that age? I know nothing uglier. The bell is calling to church, and I am happy to think I am not going. . . .

Monday, April 18. A day of settled summer weather – cool easterly breeze and a hot sun. I dreamt furiously and rose irritable. We rode to Hinton, starting 10.45. It is an unimpressive road and distant views were all blurred in haze. . . . On getting off at the station, found myself hot and slack; a pleasant, rather loquacious, young porter with Birmingham manners. Train to Ashchurch, a mysterious junction where three lines meet, and where one line goes across another almost at right angles. You can see from Ashchurch station a huge length of line – five miles, I should say, at least, quite straight. The old church looks on with melancholy over the roofs of farm buildings.

Then to Gloucester; and rode in to the Cathedral, through a murky, commercial-looking sort of town, of chimneys, and yards with piles of timber, and gas-works and ugly rows of redbrick houses. Then on turning into College Green, or whatever they call it, all is peace; and that exquisite Cathedral is surrounded by these quiet houses of infinite variety, many of them red-brick, Georgian places. A couple of thin-legged gaitered ecclesiastics, one in shovel-hat, one in square cap, were walking briskly up and down the path of the Chapter Garden. We went in, strolled about, read inscriptions, stared at statues. There is a Jenner, which though of white marble tends to convey the impression that he had a heavy cold and a red nose. There are two angels apparently squabbling over a medallion, on which is depicted a very bluff and fierce old man in high collars. ... We went round with an old, very pompous and tiresome verger, who had got his lesson by heart, and could answer no questions outside of it. I don't want to be taken round and *lectured*. I want to wander about, ask questions, and be just shown interesting things if I fail to notice them for myself.

What impressed me most of all were three tombs. Poor Edward II, looking so smooth and handsome and weak, with his delicate nose and eyes, and his carefully curled beard; then Osric, a grim old Saxon, with a shaven upper lip and archaic beard, like a Dissenting grocer. Then a noble (fifteenth century) wooden painted figure of Robert, Duke of Normandy, in mail with a red mantle, as if starting up from sleep.

I like the organ and the close screen; but the stalls are poor; and they have put in weak Gothic desks and a feeble little Throne, like a Punch and Judy show, and put the fine Jacobean woodwork into the nave, while upstairs are a few splendid corinthian columns and carved panels of fruit and flowers of a destroyed baldachino. Heart-breaking!

Mr Kempe is *everywhere* – I really begin to *hate* his glass; the same simpering faces everywhere. It seems to me that he has entirely crystallised into a tradition, and is simply turning out glass on the same lines without the slightest thought or intellectual ardour. He gave up original designing twenty years ago in favour of growing rich, I fear; while he retains the complacency of the public benefactor. . . .

We loitered about, looking at houses; went through those splendid cloisters, still all fitted for active and stately life. Then we rode off through the sunny flat to Cheltenham, the wind somewhat against us, but the bluffs of the Cotswolds looking very fine on the horizon, a church crowning a hill on the right, which rose very steeply out of the green flat. As we neared Cheltenham, we began to meet odious leisurely persons, male and female, riding together, conscious of great social superiority.

Cheltenham is a *terrible* place; its size, its respectability, its boulevards, its rows of good houses, its generally townified air, make it insupportable. Yet the bleak hills look over the house-roofs. We turned into one street and could have believed ourselves in a foreign town – a bright, broad place of white houses, with an avenue of planes; a string-band playing, little Victorias plying about, children with sunhats, a chattering crowd. It was rather pleasant.

I thought we should never get out of Cheltenham! We met among other things an old pupil of Tatham's, Ratcliff, a brewer of the neighbourhood; looking young and lusty. He asked us to call at his mother's house. Then on and on, by an electric tram-line, the outskirts getting more and more suburban, with some fine old houses engulphed; finally passed the Ratcliff's house – a noble and ancient castle! – the hill steep on our right. Then we began to ascend Cleave Hill. Passed a very charming old red-brick farm among walnuts half-way up; but new houses are perching themselves everywhere, like foul birds of prey. Still the view is *noble*: a huge wide-watered plain, full of fields, hamlets, woods and streams for miles, ending in shadowy hills. The haze dimmed and gilded it all. Gloucester tower stood out black and dark; the hill itself quite wild and down-like at the top. But there were trams ascending and descending, elderly military men taking constitutionals; wayside restaurants with people having tea; young people sporting upon the grass-grown downs. We reached the top, with its four cross-roads, and in a moment were in silence and ancient rustic peace – not a soul to be seen; but Winchcombe 800 feet below, and Sudeley Castle in its woods.

Two little things I noticed in Cheltenham which I must record: one, a complacent, red-faced, flourishing looking old gentleman, apparently in bed, at an upper window open to the street, suffering I suppose from gout, and looking most benevolently about him. The other, a very different kind of invalid, pale, worn, sunken over the temples, with lank hair; driving with his mother – he was quite a young man – she, looking so tenderly at him, said something as we passed. He frowned and shook his head. He looked *afraid*.

We rode quickly through Winchcombe, by familiar roads, and were soon comfortably at home.

Tuesday, April 19. Another beautiful day, sunny, cool, with East wind. ... There was a meet of the N.Cotswolds hounds here today; and the roads were all full of hunters – as usual Tatham met one of his boys. We rode off through Wormington and Dumbleton to Ashton-under-Hill – a pretty village, with a great old manor-house. ... We had ginger-beer at a little shop, with affectionate careful people to serve us; and then pushed up Bredon by a pleasant wooded dingle. We were soon on the bare grass fields, and struggling up through what looked like an old earthwork. Then on a long nearly flat stretch of grass, to an old tower over Woollas Hall. The hill went down quite steeply in one place, with bluffs. Elmley Castle lay nestling below, with church and lake; and we had an incomparable view over leagues of pleasant plains, full of wood, and water, and green fields and hamlets. Bredon lies isolated from all other hills and is so central that we could see Gloucester in the South West, Tewkesbury,

Pershore – and practically all the walks and rides we have taken. What a sweet and beautiful place, and how easy to live in the world looks when it lies at one's feet!

There were glints of water all over the plain – the Avon like a ribbon, the Severn like a sheet of steely blue. The hills loomed shadowy through the haze. .... We turned back and walked easily down; through a different dingle, where a bird sang sweetly, with the fragrant scent of the orchards below; and then through the orchards and past pretty nestling houses. Then we recovered our bicycles; and went by Hinton and Aston Somerville; the last an evil skulking place, not visible from anywhere, with huge new farmhouses. Took our last look at dear Buckland in its sweet combe – and so home.

Yet all this pleasant day I was melancholy and distrait; worried, so feeble are we, by my tongue, which is bad again – and oppressed with gloom. I think I am a little overtired with all this exercise; but I am otherwise very well, strong and fit, and come back after a long day in the open air with no sense of fatigue.

This has been a beautiful time here, and I have enjoyed it on the whole more than an Easter outing for many years. The great variety of things we have done and seen; the perfect weather; the coming of the Spring – all have conspired to make it beautiful and happy. I sit writing, looking out of our panelled parlour into the village street. Tatham sleeps peacefully in a chair. There is a little low stuccoed house opposite; an old lady in a cap sits all afternoon looking quietly out. She looks rosy; but the doctor goes there every day and she doesn't appear in the morning, so I suppose she is an invalid. On the right is a small, ruined, tumbledown house; on the left, the curiosity shop, with delightful chairs standing out in the street. A pleasant calm evening light over everything; and I alone seem out of tune and ill-at-ease. Partly it is the shadow of departure. I hate pulling up roots; I hate seeing the end of a delightful period. 'Oh, tis a pleasant time', as old Fitz [Edward FitzGerald] wrote, 'but it passes, passes!'

After dinner I read and wrote stupidly and heavily; then went and packed and slept with sad and ominous dreams; waked in the pale dawn by the drowsy strangled crowing of cocks – slept again – got up earlier than usual in some depression. Then finished packing, tips etc. Sent off baggage and ourselves bicycled to Evesham. It was a strange day, with so thick a haze as to be almost a fog. We went down the pretty pleasant street, and I said 'Goodbye, Broadway!' as we passed the last house. I hated going from a place where I have had a time of nearly uninterrupted happiness and pleasure. The one very striking thing as we rode into Evesham was the bloom of the orchards. Since we last rode that way all the pear and plum orchards have burst out into bloom; acres and acres are white with them. The hills, with trees in ordered rows, look like great *fleeces* – and the delicate fragrance filled the air.

[Volume 50, pp.25–78; Volume 51, pp.1–40]

X

He lunches with the Prime Minister at Whittingehame

In late August 1904, Arthur joined the Donaldsons again for a fortnight's holiday – this time at Humbie House in East Lothian, where a group of Eton and Cambridge friends, with or without their families, would assemble, for differing periods, largely for the shooting. By this time Stuart Donaldson had become Master of Magdalene, and already the idea had been mooted that Arthur, now that he was residing in Cambridge, might accept a Fellowship there (without stipend, since Magdalene was very poorly endowed). This at least is what Arthur dearly wished (indeed he had himself put forward the proposal, half-jokingly, to Stuart earlier in the year). At this stage, however, it was by no means certain that his election could be achieved without opposition. He was also a little unsettled by the rumours of Edmond Warre's imminent retirement from the Headmastership of Eton and the possibility that he might be approached to offer himself as a candidate for the vacancy.

Not far from Humbie lay Whittingehame, the family estate of Arthur Balfour, the Prime Minister. Arthur was related to him by marriage (his uncle, Henry Sidgwick, having married A.J. Balfour's sister, Nora, who became first Principal of Newnham College, Cambridge). An expedition to visit the Balfours was suggested from time to time, but Arthur was distinctly unenthusiastic. He did not like his holiday routine interrupted by social engagements, nor did he relish much being one of a party, certain members of which were only too pleased to be known to be hob-nobbing with the very eminent. He therefore hoped that somehow the expedition would be called off or conveniently forgotten. Typically, once he had bowed to the inevitable, he enjoyed the experience greatly, and wrote up the whole episode with rich and joyous detail. To set the scene, and to introduce some of the party at Humbie, I have begun the story a few days before the Whittingehame visit.

Wednesday, August 31. J.E.K.Studd[1], wife, and two boys came to lunch: and we shot at a target before. J.E.K. was at Eton and Cambridge with me. A great fanatic. He was a good cricketer and used to hold bible-classes. All the eight but two are doing some missionary work. One a soldier, one an artist. Sons of a great racing man. They all belong to the class the Scotch call the *unco guid*. J.E.K. is much improved, and is very pleasant and genial – handsome too. He devotes his whole life to Polytechnic work, and spends two months in Scotland organising tours for these young fellows, like a hotel tout. He is a very strong fellow, both in body and character – narrow-minded, of course – but rather a splendid person, who gives himself up to self-denying work. He has no sympathy with weakness or failure; doesn't want to help lame dogs over stiles. But wants everyone to be strong, ardent, good and to be converted and sing hymns in a brazen voice. He tried to get hold of the prominent and athletic polytechnicians; thinks they will leaven and lead; and neglects the rest. He has very little tenderness, I think. I liked his strong, good-natured wife and two delightful frank jolly keen boys, one at Winchester, one in the Britannia. The younger has a charming loud laugh; and took a disappointment about shooting manfully and cheerfully. The four

---

[1] Of the great cricketing family; C.T.Studd and G.B.Studd both becoming Test cricketers.

pleased me very much – so breezy, clean-limbed and clean-minded. I dare say they would bore and fret me if I had to live with them. They have not an ounce of subtlety or mystery among them.

We went on the moor and shot. I can't shoot anything on this particular moor. Had tea under some pines by a farm; and biked back.

I used to play full-back with J.E.K. for the O.E.'s in old days. He was a fierce player, knocked everyone down with a consciousness of rectitude, not kicking them in one place, but hitting them all over, and leaving them on the ground like a broken egg. He spoke approvingly of the sharp discipline of the Britannia: I felt he was hard and unmerciful about it, But then, as I say, he has *no* fellow-feeling for weakness. They were both very nice to me; pressed me to come to Polytechnic to dine etc. I was pleased at this, but shall not go.

W.Leigh[2] played a soft mournful Nocturne of Chopin's and other sweet music tonight – bright soulless things by Scarlatti; and a thing of Brahms, full of dark remoteness, which W.L. did not comprehend. Miss Cochrane[3] is too intense. She *will* try to engage me in solemn talk, when I want to giggle and make foolish jests. I am sorry for her. I slept very badly and woke aching with rheumatism. Once in the night I stood and looked into the quiet moonlit garden. How strange to think of the endless and unregarded beauty of hour after hour of moonlit nights in sweet silent cool glades!

As I write W.L. begins to play below–piercingly sweet, and my spirit goes up heavenward, reaching out somewhere, in a vague land of soft and dreamful happiness.

Thursday, September 1. . . . I was overjoyed to find the Macnaghtens at breakfast[4]. Hugh looked tired and ill, after Switzerland. Miss

---

[2] William Austen Leigh, brother of the Lower Master at Eton.
[3] A cousin of Lady Albinia (Stuart Donaldson's wife).
[4] Hugh Macnaghten, an old Eton friend, both as boy and master. He became Vice-Provost of Eton.

Macnaghten very wild and blowsy, with her eyes all twisted up. They had travelled all night. . . .

We got to Stobshields, Stuart and I, about 10.45. A nice comfortable house, among woods: with a bright garden, much out of the world, with the great bulk of Lammermuir behind. Passed Leaston, a charming house, now a farm. We went on to the moor with little Nisbet [a neighbour], whom I liked much: a simple fellow, who told us plainly that he didn't care about the bag and only wanted us to be amused. Two neighbouring squires, Fraser-Tytler and Major Gosselin (?). The latter a man with blue eyes, red moustache, a rueful glance, and a look of having been cured in smoke; but a very nice amiable fellow. F.T. fat blond lymphatic, and a really infamous shot.

Nisbet [is] one of the most *active* men I have ever seen; his little twinkling legs carried him over the moor like a Punchinello. We had some grouse drives, the last in a beck-gully near the top of Lammermuir. I was fearfully hot by the time I was at the top, scambling up the steep windless cleft with the sun on my back. But had a long delicious sit on a heather-bank while the beaters went back – a long drive; and I killed one of the two grouse I fired at. Then we went down and lunched; and Nisbet confided to me that he wouldn't go and shoot with Lord Tweeddale, because he was so much dissatisfied if the shooting was not first-rate. I always disliked Lord Tweeddale, I don't know why. Now I have reason.

Then we had a long vague walk after partridges – at first in a wide valley-basin, hidden from everything but the sky, a beautiful quiet remote place: a small wood of firs in the centre, like a temple-precinct. Here I shot a brace of hares, both sporting shots. Then we found a few partridges: and so it went on. We made up a small bag; the scenery all very pleasing, but not much view. Then tea in the comfortable house of Nisbet, looking on a glowing flower-garden. Mrs Nisbet rather pleasant; but as Lady Alba said, conversation was difficult, as you *couldn't* find any common acquaintances to discuss. Nisbet amused me much by saying that he didn't care about dress – but that the Master of Polworth gave some cause for censure by having worn riding-breeches for six years with a hole thro' which his shirt came out. 'The ladies don't like that!'

Lady Alba is excellent on these occasions – as indeed on all occasions – so simple, hearty, genial; and very amusing. She told a hysterically funny story of Lady Hobart *shrieking* into the ear of a deaf lady who had a trumpet, but who *with* the trumpet was *very* sensitive to sound. Lady Alba daredn't explain and had to sit seeing Lady H. growing exhausted by her screams and the deaf lady wincing at every word – till at last Lady H. sank back and said in a low tone (which the deaf one heard) 'You must help me, Alba – I can do no more!' at which Lady A. went off into wild giggles.

While we were away Willy Leigh went off to North Berwick in search of persons of eminence. W.L. ('dear fellow' as Wilberforce used to say when he meant to abuse someone) is clever enough to enjoy interesting talk but not clever enough to know whether talk is interesting unless it comes from a distinguished man. So he went off and found a golf tournament (the idea of going off to a golf club-house, crammed with people, when you might have seclusion, is simply *inexplicable* to me), chatted with the Prime Minister and the Colonial Secretary⁵ and Lady Frances Balfour; and talked so much about them at dinner that I said 'How dull you must find us all, after all these eminent persons' – at which a pink blush stole on to his porcelain features. But he *is* a delightful man, in spite of this very pardonable affectation.

However he brought back an invitation from Arthur Balfour to me to lunch on Saturday; and a desire appended that I would come and *stay*, if possible. This I shall be too lazy to do, of course. I should like it in one way, and I always like to feel grand; but I like my own ease and peace of mind better; and that is laziness.

H. Macnaghten is great form tonight, talking very fantastically and amusingly; but rather difficult to play up to. Miss Macnaghten is rather a terrible person. She seems to me to be entirely self-absorbed, and to study *nothing* but her own pleasure. She would

---

⁵ The Hon. Alfred Lyttelton who had recently succeeded Joseph Chamberlain in the Colonial Office.

suppose that she lived a life of simple joy. But simple joy from morning to night can only be attained by everyone else giving way to one on every point. She is very hard on Hugh. She has no mercy on him; she carries him off for a whole day – and she has very little to say. She generally looks about her like a half-awakened bird, with the nictitating membrane rising and falling over her eyes; her lips pursed up as though to whistle; her brow corrugated; and burnt the colour of a brown Toby jug.

Friday, September 2. We rode in to Tynehead, and by train to Melrose. Meanwhile Hugh Macnaghten and his sister (who rides only six miles an hour) had set off at her insistent demand to ride the whole way. They would never have got there. But Miss M. punctured, and returned. Hugh M. met us at the station. Willy Leigh, Stuart Donaldson and I rode off to Dryburgh, the rest to Abbotsford. We found it near the Tweed, not far from a fine red-scarped bend with a suspension bridge and a Greek temple with a bust of Sir Walter Scott crossing a bush-grown hillock, all befouled by tourists. The whole place very remote in some ways, but evidently much infested by sight-seers. The Abbey is rude and ancient, much of the buildings remaining which always interests me. They must have had a hard life. (N.B. Let me remember that when Abbot Forman went to see the Pope, he (Forman) told him some silly story, 'at which' says the Chronicle, 'the Pope laughed very *earnestly*'.)

I looked with reverence at Sir Walter Scott's grave. But they have filled the chapel with Taphs like a lumber-room with boxes. It is all very beautifully kept, rather finically so. The Park and mansion close at hand.

We got back to Melrose and met the rest; and mooned about the Abbey for a long time: it is now well in my head. If Melrose were situated like Dryburgh, it would be incomparably beautiful.

Then back by train: but it began to drizzle: and when we got to Tynehead with a seven-mile ride before us, it was raining hard. I had a cloak, a *casula*, and covered myself and bicycle; but we were all horribly drenched:

Then fell the floods of heaven, drowning the deep
And how my feet recrossed the deathful ridge,
No memory in me lives –

We flew up and down on muddy roads, Donald hallooing
directions to all the party, how to turn, what to avoid etc.
Unhappily in the midst of one of his shrill exhortations, he skidded
and fell on his back in the road. . . .

We were all very sleepy and tired and went to bed soon.

Saturday, September 3. The morning broke very lowering; and it
rained as I read Scott's letters in bed. With my usual pusillanimity I
was glad that I was to be spared the visit to Whittingehame. Miss
Cochrane went off: and I strolled about with Willy Leigh. I was
vexed to find that Gosse[6] had told a large party of officials at the
House of Lords all about my hope of being appointed at
Magdalene with full private details. He ought not to do this; but it
is my fault for telling him what at once becomes a secret *de
polichinelle.* Willy Leigh said to my great delight that it need not
and would not entail any separation from King's. It was pleasant in
the big ragged garden, with the huge hornbeam hedges and gleams
of sun. Miss Macnaghten flitted about like a bewildered nymph,
full of confused exalted thoughts.

About 12 it was still very threatening, raining at intervals. But
Willy Leigh came up to my room and I saw he was bent on going
to Whittingehame: a twelve-miles ride, with no chance of help
from trains if it turned out wet. I strongly deprecated it; and indeed
would not have dreamed of going as I felt sure they would not
expect us. But Hugh Macnaghten wanted to go; and Stuart
expressed a wish to go (tho' not invited) – and I felt it would be
absurd if I were to stand out; even rude. I put every difficulty in the
way, but W.L. displayed a gentle firmness coupled with high
tactical ability which was invincible.

We started at 12.30 and rode by vile sodden roads through
Gifford, an ugly naked little town, by many rolling cornlands,

---

[6] Edmund Gosse, at that time Librarian of the House of Lords.

woods and wolds to Whittingehame. I had a fall in one place, but no damage done. We went in at a nice lodge. An old man beat on the window, and – coming out – said to Hugh Macnaghten (the others were in advance) 'There is no liberty to go this way. It is private.' Hugh said meekly, 'Isn't this Mr Balfour's house? We are going to lunch with him.' Off went the man's hat, and he said 'I beg your pardon, sir.' I felt the triumphal joy of Christian meekness (that is why meekness is so pleasant, because its triumph is so much more complete). We rode a long way in a richly wooded valley with steep braes and a stream – a noble approach; and finally arrived at the house. The whole thing surprised me by its opulence and its magnificence. It is a very big, imposing house of grey stone; and the whole place trim, groomed, splendidly kept, with an air of great wealth lavishly used.

We put our bicycles by the door; and then saw the Prime Minister approaching across the grass, swinging a golf-club – in rough coat and waistcoat, the latter open: a cloth cap, flannel trousers; and large black boots, much too heavy and big for his willowy figure. He slouched and lounged as he walked. He gave us the warmest greeting, with a simple and childlike smile which is a great charm indeed. I was conscious at once of *charm* more than anything. He prattled away like a big child. 'Oh, bother this door – it always sticks.' 'Better put your bicycles round here. I was thinking of a possible horse driving up.' But everything invested with a curious grace that makes one take an almost physical pleasure in listening to him. He is a little greyer and a little stouter than when I saw him last, and has rather a worn look about the eyes, under his glasses, which melts into a naive smile, half-shy, half-caressing. He took us in; and in a big library, rather like Terling[7] – oak bookcases let into the walls, high windows, red curtains.

We found a huge family party: Lady Frances Balfour, Lady Betty Balfour, Mrs Dugdale, Lady Stepney, Aunt Nora, Arthur

---

[7] The country seat of John William Strutt, Lord Rayleigh, who was married to Evelyn Balfour, sister of the P.M. and Nora Sidgwick.

With Balfour at Whittingehame

Strutt and others. 'Here is a nephew of yours, Nora', I heard the P.M. say as we came round the screen. We went into lunch – a splendid dining-room, richly panelled in light oak, with a big piece of metal work at one end of a Burne-Jones type. But though as a rule I study the details of rooms very closely, I found today the people far more interesting. I sate next Miss Balfour and Lady Stepney. There was a saddle of mutton to carve. I offered help. 'Do you *like* carving, then? If so, you may.' 'No', I said, 'I don't – I only offered from a sense of duty.' 'Then you shall not.'

I found Lady Stepney very interesting; but I did not recognise her, though I have dined at her house in the old days (a sister of Lord de Tabley, separated from her husband, Sir —— Stepney). There were several vacant places. 'Here, what are all these places for?' said the P.M. It was pointed out that there were still several people to come; and in a minute Eustace lounged in, looking rather frightful, bloodshot, ring-straked and speckled – all the heaviness and none of the charm. Then Gerald, with his white hair, looking astonishingly handsome, in a greenish Norfolk jacket and trousers; brown boots with spats. He came up and shook hands. At lunch Eustace with much pomposity described the battles of Japs and Russians. A.B. listened politely, as if he had hardly realised there was a war going on.

I thought Miss Balfour delightful: such a sweet sisterly kind of smile; and a gracious *chatelaine* air. A pack of nice children had lunch at a separate table and were very quiet. It seems that the P.M. keeps open house thus from July to January. Gerald and Eustace let their houses, and transfer wife and children up to Whittingehame. The P.M. keeps lodgings at North Berwick for himself and goes there for golf from Monday to Friday, liking the solitary evenings. Indeed the huge family party must be a strain.

He spoke ruefully of his golf. 'My driving is getting very poor', shaking his head, but brightening up – 'but my putting was never better!'

After lunch Lady Frances came and talked to me and Mrs Dugdale, reminding me of how Willy Strutt led her in to my room at Eton and said 'This is my cousin Daffy.' 'I have been ashamed of it ever since', she went on. There was coffee in the library and Aunt Nora said to me smiling, 'If you want some, you must go and get it. No one will offer you any.'

Then the P.M. proposed a walk: he, Aunt Nora, Willy Leigh, Stuart, Hugh and myself. We strolled down towards the sea and into the valley, to a great red scarped rock. He attacked Stuart and myself and said 'I always consider that you Eton masters are *much* to blame for sending Etonians so much to Oxford. It is a national misfortune.' I talked to Aunt Nora; as we went along we found the children fishing all along the banks – long-haired girls in waders. 'They catch fish, using flies, in the *clearest* water', said A.B. 'I don't know how they do it. The habits of fish have changed very much since my day. This morning —', he went on, 'James appeared at an early hour in my bedroom with two dreadful stiffened fish which he had just caught, and said "Would you like to have them for your lunch?" – "Very much", I said, "if you only won't leave them here." He waved them in my face, laid them on the bed; and I had a horrible fear they would remain there – but he took them off at last, leaving a disgusting glutinous deposit on the door-handle, which has had to be scrubbed off with all sorts of preparations.' (I gather he was still in bed). We here separated.

Aunt Nora said that the wonderful thing about him was the absence of mental restlessness. He just changed tranquilly from one subject to another. She said that his long nights of sleep helped him very much. That is really the wonderful thing about the Balfours – the astonishing mental clearness. They are never puzzled by anything. Willy Leigh said to me, going home, that they used to be intellectually very intolerant. He said once in early days to Arthur Balfour 'The worst of your family is that you seem to think that every newcomer has the *onus probandi*, of showing that he is not a fool.' A.B. admitted it. 'But political life', said W.L., 'has rubbed it all off.' (We re-united here.)

We had some talk about preaching. 'There is such a thirst for preaching in London', he said – and about Henson.[8] Talking about

---

[8] Herbert Hensley Henson, at that stage Canon of Westminster; later Bishop of Hereford and Bishop of Durham.

the Gore and Beebee case,[9] I said rather rashly that Gore was in a painful position in having to call upon Beebee to resign for a definite offence when there was really a good deal in the background which made the resignation a necessity; and that it was unfortunate to have to call upon a man to resign and not to assign your real reasons. A.B. sighed and smiled. 'It is a position in which we politicians often find ourselves', he said. Then there followed a very interesting conversation about violence of invective, which I can only imperfectly remember. He said – I think – something to the following effect: 'I have been for thirty-five years in public life and I am constantly astonished, and increasingly so, at the extraordinary violence and vehemence of criticism which people permit themselves. Men will unhesitatingly condemn as a moral obliquity what they ought to try in the first place – and especially in the case of a friend – to believe to be only an error of judgment. I have sometimes remonstrated in cases of this kind, and have almost always been met with a frank and cordial apology – the offender evidently having no notion of the quality of his words.'

He then went on to say that what was even more strange was the way in which people heaped their bitterest denunciations on their friends. They sometimes even seem deliberately to try how much a friendship will carry in the way of denunciation.

By this time we were at the flower-garden, which is a beautiful pleasaunce, with a great wealth of flowers and shrubs, beginning with a rose-garden and a sundial. The one disadvantage is that it is separated from the house by a ravine and stream. Here we saw a gigantic yew-tree, capable of containing round its trunk in the dim gloom quite forty or fifty people. Here some treason was plotted – Darnley's murder? – all nonsense of course. Then we saw the little

---

[9] The Rev. C. E. Beeby (the correct spelling) was a liberal theologian of outspoken views within Charles Gore's diocese of Birmingham. Gore censured him for expressing doubts on the miracles, especially the Virgin Birth. He was advised against taking legal action by Sir Lewis Dibdin, but was alleged to have forced Beeby to resign by publishing a condemnation of his views in his Diocesan magazine.

red tower, with Douglas arms, that is the original fortress of the mansion. Here Miss Balfour has a big room, with a handsome Jacobean ceiling and some good china, bought in a cottage.

We lingered back. I walked with Gerald who talked very amiably about the Queen's letters, recurring at intervals to the Board of Trade.[10] Then we made haste to go; shook hands with the pleasant simple family group; and rode up the curving drive and out of sight.

The weather was now fine and warm. We had a quick ride home, Willy Leigh and I going by the ancient road, Stuart and Hugh Macnaghten taking a new route, and arriving long after us.

What I am struck with, in reflecting about this very pleasant and interesting visit is (1) the magnificence of the house etc. It is a big place and very well kept up. (2) The extraordinary simplicity and kindness of the Premier. Who could believe that this childlike naive smiling man, with just a touch of the spoilt child in his voice, moving about, a little bowed, a little shambling, with apparently nothing to do but loaf about and talk to his visitors could be the Premier? So many men of big position would have been civil enough to a set of nobodies at lunch; but to spend the whole afternoon in that most dismal and tiring and yawn-engendering of all occupations – viz. to lounge about your own place with a party of visitors; and to exhibit nothing but a profound contentment, or at least gentle acquiescence, this is indeed a model of chivalry if not of Christian grace.

I was immensely struck by his *charm*, which adds a kind of glow to the simplest things he says. Gerald has not got this – still less Eustace with his marred and rueful visage. Miss Balfour has it in some degree; but without the trenchant wit or quick perception. Aunt Nora is like a little Abbess ... communing with the skies, but delighted if one will only ramble on.

Willy Leigh, on the return home, told an interesting story how he dined with Arthur Balfour and Henry Sidgwick (before the marriage) and how A.B. confessed himself to be a sceptic in the

---

[10] Gerald Balfour was President of the Board of Trade in Balfour's cabinet.

With Balfour at Whittingehame

presence of political economy and philosophy and history and everything – but that he still held orthodox views in religion; and in politics would support the Church of England thro' thick and thin. Henry Sidgwick said, with a little stammer, that *he* would support it only through thin; but presently confessed that an attitude of general scepticism combined with a certain orthodoxy of religious belief was not an uncommon thing among his pupils.

A quiet evening and early to bed – after a really very interesting day ... I very nearly had a bad accident ... at Whittingehame. We were riding carelessly, three abreast down the drive. I slipped just close to a low parapet with a steep brae below – very nearly overbalanced. If I had fallen I must have been killed. There came into my head the whimsical thought that it would have been strange when E.W.B. had died at Hawarden, if I had died at Whittingehame! ...

[Volume 58, pp. 15–43]

XI

◇

He samples episcopal magnificence at Farnham Castle

Later in September 1904 Arthur had a short spell at Tremans, the house at Horsted Keynes in Sussex where his family now lived. He was joined by one of his closest Eton friends, Francis Warre Cornish, a quiet, gentle scholar, several years Arthur's senior, who was then Vice-Provost of Eton. Often enough Arthur and Cornish had spent afternoons at Eton walking and talking together, as the spirit moved them. On the occasion recorded here, the combination of a perfect setting, clement weather and the consciousness of relaxed friendship provided exactly the right mood for an intimate exchange to develop quite naturally without being forced or laboured. The whole episode had for Arthur what he described as 'the quality of memorability, without which no felicitousness of weather or companion or talk can give a day permanence of recollection'.

From Tremans he went to stay with another old Eton friend, Herbert Ryle, who had recently become Bishop of Winchester, succeeding Randall Davidson on his elevation to the primacy. At the time Arthur had counselled Ryle not to accept because he had been too short a time at Exeter as bishop, and it might have been felt that he had given way to ambition in moving to one of the premier sees, with its magnificent episcopal residence at Farnham Castle. To Winchester, however, Ryle went; and was taken ill very shortly afterwards with *angina pectoris*. He asked Arthur to come and see him and to spend a night or two at the Castle. His son, Edward, would be at home, having left Eton (where he had been Arthur's last House Captain), and was shortly to go up to Cambridge. The family were worried about his passion for sport and the not unlikely possibility that he would shirk his studies.

It was not the first time that Arthur had stayed at Farnham, but he had never before been so much struck by its opulence and palatial atmosphere. How long would a Prince of the Church be able, or willing, to maintain such state? Even Arthur, with his memories of Lambeth and Addington Palace, was conscious that he was witness to, if not the ending of an epoch in the history of the Anglican Church, at least its twilight hours.

Friday, September 16. I spent a vague morning; strolling with the Vice-Provost, reading, writing and so on. In the afternoon I went a very memorable walk with him. It was very hot; and everything lay in a golden haze which intensified and did not hide the sweet distance. We went by Masetts and the Sloop right up to the North Common, all purple and gold with heather and yellow flowers. Then back by Scaynes Hill. The views all incomparably rich and dim; but so beautiful! I never loved the earth better. What remains with me is a green alley in a wood, very long and straight, all tapestried with leaves and broken light – a rabbit hopping across.

Then the beautiful water-meadows below East Mascalls, the evening sun just gilding outlines and casting long shadows – an incommunicable peace over all. The meadows full of tall plants, giving that effect of double surfaces; the long flat meadows, with thorn trees and alders, with the wooded slopes each side; and a glint of blue hills beyond. But *why* does one love it all so much? And what does that love mean?

We talked of many things – of books and activities and death and faith. He told me, in confidence, that he had been co-opted to the Governing Body for life. I was glad of this, for he certainly would not have been re-elected; and who will succeed him? Walter Durnford, I suppose. Then of the Headmastership and we discussed possibilities. We added Alington[1] to the list. He is a strong fellow, but wants manner and mellowness. He is rather a chatterbox too. I should like him a few years hence.

We sate for some time on the heather slopes looking North. I must not forget the broken lock-gate and the sprouting alders by the Sloop Inn. The day was somehow filled to the brim with peace, with gentle reverie. I liked my companion. He is a wise tender man. I wish he had been a little more successful; but that is the stuff of the man, I think. He has some genius. And he keeps an open, just and youthful mind. Who, of the young bucks, would have discussed books with such zest and perception? There is no solemnity or priggishness about him either. . . .

In our talk this afternoon we rejected the idea of *Sacrifice* in the Redemption. Sacrifice is, I believe, a *merely* savage idea. Propitiation of a more or less hostile power. He told me that Rashdall[2] etc. have been discussing whether God's laws are self-imposed or imposed from outside. This seems to me very futile. If they are from outside, then the Power that imposes them is what I mean by God – the *ultimate essence*. . . . The Vice-Provost dwelt upon metempsychosis – to me a horrible idea. For a man to go thro' the world, slide at last into the weariness of age; with all the gain of character, mellowness, affection, faith; and then to begin again with all the wretched incidents of infancy, the dependence, the birth of sin, the facing of the world. It is so horribly undignified! It may be true, of course; but what a misery if one believed it.[3]

---

[1] The Rev. Cyril Alington, recently appointed Master in College at Eton. He became Headmaster of Shrewsbury in 1908 and succeeded Edward Lyttelton as Head Master of Eton in 1916.
[2] Hastings Rashdall, the leading spirit of liberal 'modernist' theology.
[3] A.C.B. was to change his mind on this quite radically. In *The Child of the Dawn* (1912), a sort of eschatological novel, he was to express a firm belief in reincarnation.

Episcopal magnificence at Farnham Castle

How strange it is that the thought that all men have died or will die does not reconcile one in the least to Death. One thinks of one's ancestors' death as a harmless, necessary, almost pleasant incident in their lives!

The walk with the V.P. keeps on recurring to my mind. It somehow has the *quality of memorability* without which no felicitousness of weather or companion or talk can give a day permanence of recollection.

Saturday, September 17. It was a very bright and delicious morning. I packed and went off to Farnham. I got to town at 1.30. A beautiful fresh day, full of life and sun. Drove to the National, deposited things; and on to Oxford and Cambridge Club (the Athenaeum being closed). Here I met Childers[4] who came up on purpose. We had a good careful talk about many small details, and looked up some minute points in the Library. We lunched in a large secluded room, looking out to Marlborough House, which I believe is called *Aceldama*, the place to *bury strangers in*. Then we walked thro' Park, looked at the flowers and aquatic birds, notably the pelicans, who looked like swans muffled up for sore-throat. I showed Childers over the National Club; had tea and off to Waterloo. The country very beautiful, in a rich golden light. I always like the heather and fir-land – the forest tracts are however sadly invaded by rows of new red houses. It always brings back the old Wellington days to me.

The good Edward [Ryle] met me at Farnham station; we walked up; he was very full of a visit to Walter Pollock, who seems to have overcome his failing, and to live in a little house crammed with souvenirs. The Castle looked very splendid, towering up above the town – which is in itself a very contented happy-looking little place, with its red-brick houses and white window-casements.

We went in at once to see Herbert; and I was much relieved and delighted to see him just his old self; still very brown with the sun,

---

[4] Hugh Childers, whose help Arthur had enlisted with the Queen Victoria letters.

but with the same good-natured easy affectionate tranquillity. A sort of calm and sensible content always seems to brim over from him. He looked really quite robust, and I was glad to be able to tell him sincerely that I should not have guessed he had been ill, which cheered him visibly. Presently Mrs Ryle came in, very warm and welcoming; looking tired and haggard but with a good colour. I now like her little prim peremptory ways, which I used to think trying. What a difference it makes when one *knows* a person likes one. Edward stayed while we talked; silent but smiling. He too looks quite his old self.

Herbert led me presently to my bedroom – a great big comfortable room; with a Morris paper, the pattern much too large – no restfulness. I forgot to say that we were received at the door by butler and two footmen. It is all rather stately – a rich and sober state. Butler and three footmen wait noiselessly and attentively at *all* the meals, and do not go till Herbert gives them a grave signal.

It is a very noble house – the huge hall with its big balustrades, and the wealth of rich carving making it abundantly picturesque. All the appointments very smart. We dined magnificently in the big hall; a Miss Synge the only other guest: quaint-looking, but a very sweet-tempered serious person, I think. She works for the Charity Organisations in town.

After dinner we smoked in the Hall; and then arrived Dr Ryle, Herbert's brother, only a year older, but looking ten years his senior. One of those men who one sees has crystallised into certain silly rules of dress etc. at an early age. A very low collar, red tie, ugly boots; a white beard and rather bald: an uninteresting well-meaning man. Then we had chapel, Herbert reading; the chaplain away. I was glad to see that the odd raucous pronunciation, which I think he must have unconsciously adopted from Temple, seems to be subsiding. He seems now only to fall into it when he thinks of it. He is not a good reader, somehow. He wore his Garter ribbon at dinner, and looked every inch a gracious and dignified prelate. The chapel is very delightful; but I cannot say the seats are comfortable. They have taken away the altar-picture, and the plants which used to stand by the altar (and which I intensely disliked) embowering it.

Then we smoked a little more in the study; but Herbert to bed. I liked to sit there under the grave picture of Fox [Bishop of Winchester, 1501–28], very lean with downcast eyes. The pictures are the worst part of Farnham. Not very many and several of them bad copies; and such a stodgy set of men: Morley, the great builder of Farnham and the ascetic, in that dreadful Charles I style with dank hair over his forehead, looking like a man after a night of dissipation.

Sunday, September 18. I slept very ill, as I always do in a strange house and rose tired. There was an early celebration. The bad point here is the infernal punctuality. The time is some minutes fast, and Mrs Ryle said that she was herself so punctual, that the servants were apt to ring the bells too soon. She seemed pleased at this; but it makes it very uncomfortable for guests.

I was accordingly late; came in after the Decalogue. They sang 'Bread of Heaven' very sweetly; a spectacled maid having a clear pure voice and delicate phrasing. Mrs Ryle played organ, but without pedals.

Then breakfast; and soon after walked to Church. The morning very fresh and fine. It surprised me to see how very few people greeted Herbert in the street; and his own salutations were not cordial – rather absent-minded. The Church is fine; a cruciform place. I well remember the Xmas service here in 1896, when I spent Xmas here, the others being all abroad. *How* tired I was! The singing was good; a B.Mus. organist; but a horrible man screeched behind us. The whole place had a rich local feeling; the Churchwarden with Dundreary whiskers heading the procession of alms-bags; everyone exactly appraised by everyone else.

Herbert was in robes; he walked in very nobly attended by the churchwardens with maces – very unlike the guilty way in which Randall [Davidson] used to creep in, with rolling eyes, and uneasy glances in all directions, as tho' he were a thief expecting to see a detective in one of the seats. My old acquaintance, O'Rorke, is

Vicar. Gardiner has been extravagant and must retrench, so he resigns. O'Rorke preached a very weak sermon, about the Widow's son – no thought, no colour. It was here that I saw the dirty old lady sing 'Join the triumph of the skies' – today she was gone.

After church we walked in the Park, Dr Ryle without a hat. It is a fine place. We discussed the possible sale of it. Herbert says that it would hardly be worth while to sell it under £200,000. The expenses are enormous – four gardeners etc. But the Park is absolutely open to the public; and no millionaire would care to buy that. It seems that Cardinal Vaughan wanted to buy it. I rather wish he had. I think that a place like this is absurd nowadays. It was all very well when a Bishop was a real territorial magnate, with a huge income. But now he is in a false position. I think that they ought to have dignity; but it should be purely ecclesiastical dignity. The income does not really suffice to keep up state; and Farnham demands state. It is rather a sham kind of dignity.

We strolled round the Keep: like a great crag, full of bushes and climbing plants – most beautiful. The gardens very trim. Then we watched the goldfish, turned on fountain and at last went into lunch. After lunch a long slow pleasant walk to Caesar's Camp. I had a careful talk with Herbert about Edward. There is no anxiety, I am glad to find. Edward will eventually have £1000 a year from his grandfather. Herbert is very wise and hopeful about him. I had an interesting talk too to Miss Synge about *Hill of Trouble, Rossetti*[5] etc. But I think I talked too much.

The view over the great forest plain most noble – all dark and dusky with firs and heather. I could just see the twin peaks of Ambarrow and Edgebarrow by Wellington. It gave me a strange half-sweet heartache. Almost all we could see was Herbert's diocese. He seemed to have a kind of pride in that.

Tea. Herbert was tired and lay down. Then I went and had a long pathetic talk with Mrs Ryle. She is very tired, very anxious

---

[5] A.C.B.'s book on Rossetti has been referred to before. *The Hill of Trouble*, published by Isbister in 1903, was a collection of supernatural tales originally told to Eton boys.

and I fear very unhappy. We talked long about Edward. She is now convinced that she must leave the *details* of his life alone, and stick to principles only; but it will be very difficult, for her mind turns so much to details, e.g. she expressed a hope he would attend the University Sermon at Cambridge! I could not re-echo it. I pressed with all my might the view that insistence on details is the cause of half the sad misunderstandings between parents and children; the fashion of the world changes, and little trifles (such as smoking etc.) which were against the principles of the older people, and stood for laxity of practice, become a regular concomitant of life for all. We were interrupted by an incursion of Miss Faithfulls, who belong to the peculiar type of woman which gathers round episcopal residences, and rush in full of goodness, with nothing much to say, but all aglow about saying it.

Still I had an interesting talk about art with one of them. Mrs Ryle seemed to want me to stop on (we were in her own sitting-room), so I stopped till it was time to dress. She recurs at intervals pathetically to carpets and china and the duties of the third footman. But she is a gallant and loyal little woman and I am really fond of her. I sign myself to her 'Yours affectionately' with real sincerity. She rebuked me for saying 'the Bishop'. 'That sounds so unnatural from you.'

Dinner; many footmen – not much talk. Herbert is reading a great deal of poetry. That is good. He wants poetry. He went to bed early; and I talked drearily enough to Dr Ryle about Repton and schools in general. Edward to bed, having to play at the Oval tomorrow. I slept a little better.

Monday, September 19. I was late for prayers. Edward went off. We had a pleasant breakfast and a little talk, like old friends. I tipped largely, and went off in state with a footman to hand me to the train. It was such a beautiful and bright day that I gave up all idea of trying to do odd jobs in town (and the Athenaeum is closed), and flew to Victoria; caught the Seaford express, and walked up from the station, glad to be at home. But also very glad to have been at Farnham. Herbert touched me much by saying 'You don't know how much your visit had cheered and helped us.' I think he was particularly alluding to this. I had told him about my Professorship[6] and why I had refused. A little later he began to talk about his own leaving Exeter; so I saw that something pricked him. So I said frankly that I must tell him that I had heard his appointment to Winton much canvassed, but never a *word* to imply that he had acted from worldly motives – but even the fear of that being said, I added, ought not to come in when one thinks one is doing right. How much better it is to say out what is in one's mind. He was thinking no doubt of the strong letter I wrote to him urging him to refuse Winchester.

[Volume 59, pp. 19–36]

---

[6] Arthur had been offered the Professorship of English Literature at 'the Yorkshire University' at Leeds at a salary of £600 p.a. He had turned it down.

XII

◇

He spends Christmas at Claremont with the Duchess of Albany

Royal commissions to write odes and hymns for the Court brought Arthur from time to time into court circles. Not unnaturally, then, he was chosen to be the Housemaster, at Eton, of the young Duke of Albany, grandson of Queen Victoria and only son of Prince Leopold (created Duke of Albany) and Helena, Princess of Waldeck-Pyrmont. Prince Leopold died in 1884, the year in which his son, Charles Edward, was born; and Helena was left a widow with an infant daughter, Alice (later Countess of Athlone), only one year older than her newly-born brother. Albany's stay at Eton was very short. In July 1899, it was arranged – at the Queen's command – that the boy should leave for Germany on his succession to the Duchy of Saxe-Coburg, where he was to be brought up by German tutors. It was a sad parting, and the boy kept in touch with his Housemaster for several years. Arthur also stayed on three or four occasions with the Duchess of Albany at Claremont near Esher in Surrey to discuss her son's affairs and to advise her about his upbringing as best he could. On these occasions he would invariably meet the young Princess Alice for whom he developed a very great affection. In 1904 Princess Alice married Alexander, Prince of Teck. Arthur attended the wedding and shortly after went to lunch with the young couple informally at Windsor. At Christmas that year, a great family gathering was planned. The Duke was to come over from Coburg and expressed the wish that Arthur should be there. Rather dreading the prospect of living at close quarters with royalty on a festive occasion, Arthur reluctantly agreed. He would spend Christmas at Claremont, travelling from Windsor by car with Princess Alice; take a short break with his own family at Tremans; and then return to Claremont to see Albany whose visit was delayed. When it came to the point (as happened so often before) he found that he enjoyed the occasion far more than he had expected. But it was not an experience that he wished to repeat. Although he was himself to entertain the Duchess of Albany later at Cambridge, he never visited Claremont again.

With this visit, a chapter in Arthur's life effectively closed. Eton, with Windsor Castle nearby, ceased to be the centre of his life as he moved into Magdalene and indulged his passion for reflective musings 'from a College window', 'beside still waters', from his 'silent isle'. This episode, then, forms a fitting finale to this selection of early Edwardian vignettes.

Friday, December 23. Woke in much depression. Morning – a horrible fuss packing etc. Heavy fog. Got to Castle and wrote many letters and a few paragraphs of the book.[1] Childers late. I was weary, but the writing put me right. Then at 1.30 I went by appointment to lunch with the Tecks, and met them like old friends. I ought to use ceremony but can't. We had a good lunch; and then went off at 2.45 in a fine big smooth-running motor. Sentries saluting and police very solemn. I sate behind with the Princess who wrapped me in furs; she in the highest spirits at going home and with the fresh air. We talked and giggled like two relations – uncle and niece. She looked very charming in her furs with a fine colour in her cheeks. It only took an hour, on sloshy roads with dim-veiled trees and houses; we went by Staines and

---

[1] A.C.B. was still working, with Hugh Childers, on the Queen Victoria letters.

Walton – passing Mount Felix; and soon flew in at the great gates. We made rather an ugly skid in the park, but the chauffeur was very skilful. The Duchess appeared at the door with Lady Collins[2] – and I had a very warm welcome.

I find Alex of Teck a very congenial person – full of humour and talk and interest in people. He has that curious royal vivacity which is characteristic and convenient. The Princess is not the least like a married woman, but like a very simple and merry girl.

We all went in to the Duchess' room and talked. Then Collins and Raper,[3] looking funnier than ever, like a very damaged Dickens, arrived. Raper was even more shy and awkward than myself. The Duchess talked to me about Albany and the great disappointment it was that he couldn't come home yet, owing to the death of the old Duchess of Coburg. All the Xmas festivities postponed.

Collins took me to my room – a huge gorgeous apartment, looking out in front, lit with many lustres. I am told I may smoke here. Then we had tea in the saloon, a jolly merry meal. Then we went to Collins' room, who showed me a lot of very interesting letters – Ruskin, Creighton, Myers, Goldwin-Smith etc. Teck and Raper came in and we gossiped about Eton and the Headmastership. And then I went to my apartment – I can't call it a room – where I wrote a few letters and diary.

Of course I am a little oppressed – but how silly to be so shy and apprehensive of this pleasant easy family party. One's comfort really depends on how one feels. When one is brisk and lively, it is all right. But then comes a mild day and all the stiffening melts out. I am to go back to Tremans on Monday; and then to return here on Thursday to see the Duke. Who could be anything but pleased at such a welcome and such faithful friendship? ... I have a nice grave, respectful young footman in scarlet to wait on me. This would have appalled me in former days. But I am now so used to it at the Castle that it seems normal.

---

[2] Wife of Sir Robert Collins – see below.
[3] Sir Robert Collins, equerry to the Duchess of Albany. Raper, Fellow of Trinity College, Oxford, was another guest.

At Claremont with the Duchess of Albany

As usual I had forgotten to bring my medal[4] and found Teck and Collins gorgeous with orders and stars. We had a very pleasant dinner, I taking in Lady Collins – all very simple and merry – a bottle of Lafitte and some ancient sherry produced in my honour, as I am much bantered on my abstemiousness. Then after dinner we went to the saloon and sate down to play Bridge. Teck and I played the Duchess and Raper. We held all the cards, and I found myself to my amazement the best player. Then we went off to the library and smoked; and Teck and I had a real Eton gossip and told stories till all was blue. Bed, very sleepy, at 12.30; but I slept well and peacefully, for a wonder, though wakeful about dawn.

Saturday, December 24. Breakfast at 9. Very late – it seems they are not punctual here. It was dark and foggy outside, so we had the big red lamp over the table lit. Then to the library, where the Duchess, standing, had a long talk to me. I hate standing but survived. And then settled down on me that peculiar kind of weariness that comes on in strange houses where I can't follow my own devices. I read the papers; and then Teck, Collins and I went off through the misty park, where Collins exhibited great agility, jumping fences etc., to Dr Royle, who with his wife and daughters received us, offered cherry brandy etc., by me refused. Royle was Prince Leopold's doctor, rather like Robert Browning. Then we went on to Esher old Church, now deserted. The only absolutely untouched old place, high pews, galleries etc. The old royal pew a kind of gallery, which the Queen loved, and fireplaces. The carving much broken off by curio-hunters. We explored the whole place, tower, galleries etc. – I wish it could be preserved; but it is not big enough, and is getting dilapidated. The exterior most nondescript, with odd additions, chimneys, dormers etc. But it must be a real curiosity. Back to lunch, a kind of *Mittags-Essen*, much too long. Then we turned over a portfolio of old scraps off a screen belonging to Princess Charlotte – Bartolozzis, Gillrays etc. all horribly snipped.

---

[4] The Coronation Medal, awarded in recognition of the Coronation Ode.

At Claremont with the Duchess of Albany

Then I walked down with the Duchess to the farm, and had a very interesting talk about the Queen. She told me of her first quarrel with her. The Queen had settled that the Duchess was to have a particular maid; the Duchess wanted to keep her own. 'At last', said the Duchess, 'I lost my temper, flounced into the Queen's room and said I would not have my personal servants settled for me behind my back; that I might have done it, if I had been asked, not otherwise.' 'Most improper', said the Queen. But the Duchess found that she got her own way and the Queen said 'I can do nothing with the Duchess; she is very disobedient; but unfortunately in this case she is quite right. It is what I should have done myself.' From this dated their close friendship. 'The Queen was never rude to me, and she was often rude to the others. She thought me sincere and straightforward and trusted me, telling me all she thought. But we had frequent quarrels. Once when my husband was ill in bed, the Queen, who asked his advice about everything – he took the Prince Consort's place – said he must read her boxes as usual and make notes. I said to the Queen that he must do no such thing, but must try to sleep. "You spoil him", she said. "It will do him good." I said that I would not argue it, but if the boxes came in I would carry them out with my own hands. "What right have you to say that?" said the Queen. "He is my husband, ma'am." The Queen smiled, "Well, you spoil him." She was very hard on Prince Leopold. She made him useful to her and never gave him any freedom. She would not allow him to become a Peer for a long time, unless he would promise that he would not make the House of Lords an excuse for running up to town.'

She went on to say that it was *his* death which altered the Queen. She was hard and severe before, and then became tender and sweet. She never quite forgave herself for the way she had treated him, and for forgetting his infirmities. The Queen was a curious mixture of great bluntness and great desire not to hurt peoples' feelings. The Duchess related to me a long story of the Queen's diplomacy to get her to make a change in her morning. At last the Duchess went straight to the Queen and said; 'Why don't *you* speak to me direct about these things, instead of doing it through half-a-dozen feelings?' 'I thought you would be vexed.' Then after a pause the Queen said 'If I only had had someone who could have talked plainly to *me*, when I was left a widow, I should have been spared much unhappiness.'

At the farm there was a pretty sight. The men on the estate came one by one, and each received a bit of beef from the Duchess' own hands with a few kind words. Very feudal and simple. It was amusing to see her being led away afterwards to wash her greasy hands by the Princess, who held up her train.

The Princess was delightful. So gay and full of life – and just like a girl still. I like the relations of the pair – and I like Teck more and more – so kind and simple. He is a really interesting fellow to talk to. Then we went, Collins, Teck, Raper and I, through misty pinewoods by strange frozen lakes, and through rhododendron walks, the day darkening. Teck and I discussed the Army, management of subalterns, mess questions. I find him a very pleasant companion – very straightforward and very ready to be amused.

Then Collins came and took us round the great vaulted kitchens, like a monastery – fine rooms for Steward, Housekeeper etc., all full of fine old chairs. I like Collins' way with the servants, so kind and paternal. He is a truly delightful man – full of poetry, which he quotes very feelingly. Last night, I forgot to say, he was in a freakish mood. He first knocked down a whole pile of pictures by accident; and then, finding his party dull, began to play the fool charmingly. He stood quoting poetry, with a large wooden coal-scuttle on his head, like a German grenadier. It was incredibly ludicrous, and everyone went into hysterics. But all without any affectation or loss of dignity. He is a perfect man in the place. I like his low, distinct voice; his smile, his charming unobtrusive manners.

We had tea – less and less formality; and the Duchess talked interestingly about languages and how she thought in them. Then all slipped away – and I had a curious grave talk with Raper about Eton. He said that he had an object in speaking because he had heard (from Sir William Anson, I gathered) that at all events one section of the Governing Body had made up their minds to offer it to me. This brings the horrible decision closer. Raper said, smiling 'You will have to resign all hopes of immortality and give up your best and most productive years.' I explained to him my position. He said 'Well, there is much to be said on both sides.'[5] Then he talked interestingly about Pater[6] – Jowett's hospitality; and said that Pater had been scared out of excessive aestheticism by a sermon of Mackarness's [Bishop of Oxford] against him.

Raper told me a curious story. He believes that Newman's election, at his own suggestion, to an Hon. Fellowship at Trinity, was the ultimate cause of his Cardinalship, owing to the stir it made in Roman circles.

He is an interesting and high-minded man; a little *queer* in some ways. But with great sympathy and perception. Since then I have been quietly reading, writing and smoking in my room; much more at ease than I was yesterday. I have never before been on such *easy* terms with these people.

Several neighbours to dinner: The Royles and Wightwicks. More court dress than ever, Royle in kneebreeches, and both Teck and Collins respendent with ribbons and collars; Princess Alice in sapphires with nodding diamonded rays on her head, like the antennae of a butterfly. I took in Mrs Royle – a handsome vivacious woman; and sate next Mrs Wightwick. We *drew* for partners and places. It was a very German kind of meal – little Xmas trees on the table, covered with cotton wool and strings of little glass beads to represent frozen gossamers. Dinner was quite uneventful, except that some old malmsey was produced, of which Mr Raper spoke in exaggerated praise. It tasted to me merely like old soft sweet sherry.

Then I had a little talk to Royle and the Prince; and then we went to the drawing-room. Here one of those curious little scenes

---

5 A.C.B. would have liked the outright offer of the Headmastership of Eton. In the end he played too difficult to get. While he recognised this, he still felt rather that he had been snubbed.

6 A.C.B. had begun work on a study of Walter Pater for the *English Men of Letters* series.

occurred that shows the odd fondness that Royalty have for 'ragging' other people and laughing at their discomfiture, when they are sure they will never be made to look foolish themselves. (Compare, the King of Portugal cramming handfuls of snow down the necks of his staff at Windsor and hurling huge snowballs at them; they in return making up snow-balls of the size of marbles and throwing them gingerly back, taking care to miss.) Someone had put up some mistletoe under the chandelier. Teck (who is always ragging Lady Collins) dragged her beneath, and Royle kissed her! Very vulgar, very harmless; but stupid too and out of date. The Royalties screamed with laughter. But if Mr Wightwick and I had dragged the Duchess underneath and embraced her, how would she have liked it? It would have been 'a liberty'. Well, why is it not a liberty with Lady Collins? Because of the d——d feeling that makes horseplay from a Royalty into a piece of gracious condescension. That is why I couldn't bear to live among them.

Then we all settled down in a circle: the Duchess opened a huge parcel, and parcels were distributed all round. But one's parcel contained two more, addressed to other people; and when one's new parcels came, there again were more belonging to others. At last we were all sorted out. With the ultimate parcels came *rhymes*, some by the Duchess, some by Collins, which were really quite good. I received a little oak clock and a paperweight – a silver skate lying on a block of crystal, like ice – both belonging to Prince Leopold.

Then we played round games – more intelligently than I could have supposed. I was sent out and had to question the circle, which was rather terrible. We went on till late; and it was all hearty, simple, friendly and German. A certain amount of simple ragging, for which I haven't the animal spirits. Smoked, and went to bed late.

Sunday, Christmas Day. I was called early, in the dark; and for a minute could not remember where I was. Then I came out of the tide of sleep. I was dressed by 8.0; and found the Duchess, Princess and ladies waiting in the Hall. Collins waited to bring on Teck. I was equipped with keys and prayer-books. We walked through the silent misty shrubberies, in the cool fresh air – the little bell beating in the mist below. The Duchess and Princess walked first, talking in low tones, of things religious, I think. There was a certain solemnity about it. Collins and the Prince caught us. We went to the little tin church at West End: a horrid little place – the party filled three seats – a simple service well read (tho' rather monotonously) and too long. Then back to breakfast. This was all rather a fuss; but I found a nice little Xmas card on my plate from the Princess.

Then we walked off to church at Esher. I with the Prince later. Raper apparently wouldn't go. We hurried; and were late for the procession. The Claremont Pew is a *room*, Turkey-carpeted, and with a noble tapestry on one side, with a desk and comfortable arm-chairs overlooking the choir, so that one is on a level with the organ-pipes opposite. The choir were in their places. There followed an interesting service, the music well selected, the choir evidently well trained, and the organ splendidly played, tho' with perhaps a little too much agility. The man moved about so much, and shut off stops like a monkey in a cage. But his taste was great and the 'colour' good. A fine organ. He accompanied the Athanasian Creed nobly.

The sermon was dull and I fell asleep. I learnt afterwards that I had snored! The Prince ought to have awakened me, and I reproached him. He said, 'Oh, I told you he would send you to sleep – besides you looked so comfortable.' For the offertory a side-door in the panelling was opened; and the sidesman came up a staircase.

Then we all went in state and inspected the decorations of the fire-engine and engine-house, which is very carefully done at Xmas. We were received by a guard of saluting firemen etc. The place was elaborately decorated in a childish sort of way. How wonderful the pleasure people will take in *handiworks* of this hideous kind, who would never look at a sunset or a wood in spring.

I walked back with Collins, and we met the organist; a young enthusiastic fellow, not quite a gentleman. But my criticisms were justified as I find he is assistant-organist at the Chapel Royal. I had particularly noticed the boys and how well they managed their *lips* – and this I found to be a great idea of his.

Then came lunch – all rather weary; and then I looked with Collins over a lot of the Queen's old child's-books; well-bound and fine editions, but oh, what sad stuff. We found an old hymn-book belonging to Georgiana Harcourt, of Bishopthorpe, Loulou's grandmother, which I despatched by Collins' request to him. Then we went off for a walk – the Prince, the Princess, Miss Potts, Collins and myself. The Duchess went away to sleep, I think. She is much stouter than she used to be, and looks to me more phlegmatic and somnolently inclined.

We went through the Park and by the pretty West End common, which looked very beautiful in the mist, breaking away to the flat ground. We entered one of the most hideous gardens I have ever seen – horribly and abominably neat, and without a particle of taste, in which stood one of the most hideous houses I have ever seen. Not old. This was tenanted, Collins told me, by an old retired stockbroker, who was an old and faithful friend – his name, I think, McClostie? – very rich, rather eccentric. He called one day and said he would like to make Albany and Princess Alice birthday presents, in return for all the Duchess' kindness etc. He was permitted, and gave them each a cheque for a thousand pounds – *which was accepted*!

As we walked past the dining-room window, we saw him at a table in the window writing. We saw him and he saw us; but it would not have been consistent with good manners to receive us so: so when we got in he was sitting in the drawing-room on a sofa, reading an elegantly-bound volume. He must have *run*!

The room was almost incredibly hideous and neat. It must have been furnished in the sixties – grey paper shot with gold; maroon curtains and sofas; frightful ornaments; everything thin and tawdry. A bust of McClostie in the corner with large side-whiskers and a toga. But the old man was splendid fun; it was simply as good as a play to see him: very ugly, very jolly, a broad Scotch accent; no respecter of persons, and full of pawky humour. Miss Potts, who is a faded, rather red-nosed, frigid looking thin woman said that McClostie never came to see her (she has a cottage near). McClostie with an ineffable look rallied her on the danger he would run. 'We young fellows', he said, 'and highly inflammable too' (he is 85, and hideous) 'have to keep a course far from the Isles of the Sirens', and so on.

He greeted me very warmly, held my hand for some time in his soft palm, asked after my wife, and could not be persuaded I was not married. 'Why, I sate next her', he said, 'at the Confirmation of the Duke.'

This visit was a *great* amusement to me; and the enjoyment of the Princess in the old fellow was delightful to see – and his tenderness and fatherliness to her. 'Well, Prince – and how's the sojering?' was his greeting to Teck. The old man has lost his wife lately, and has no friends; he was spending an absolutely lonely Xmas in this horrible house, yet in *high* good humour and spirits. I wonder how he filled up the day!

We walked back through the Park. I saw an odd-looking Gothic building through a vista of rhododendrons and asked Teck what it was. He suggested going to see it. So we went. It was a kind of mausoleum (only a cenotaph, of course) built by the King of the Belgians to Princess Charlotte, in the worst Gothic of 1820 or thereabouts. But all so pathetically careful, and the stained glass really *excellent* of its kind. But all neglected. Hoes and garden rollers kept there, and the Princess's bust with a moustache and imperial pencilled by a garden-boy. One of the pretty little panes was lying shattered on the ground. I suppose it was a kind of sentimental place, to go and sit and meditate on Charlotte's constancy – and then, I suppose, the good Prince went off to the mistress who lived at West End, brought there by Stockmar, the virtuous Stockmar! There was a fine dim view of falling slopes, broken woods, and vistas from the place – some old childish gardens – the Duke's and Princess's.

We went a long ramble all about the grounds, which were laid out by Capability Brown, but the old terraces etc. are all grown up and lost, the temples rotting away; no money, I fear, to keep it going. Visited the great Folly Tower, and saw the children's little fort there. It is a very beautiful and attractive place, but too much embowered in rhododendrons. It would do best for a very rich statesman's villa, for week-end political parties – not enough shooting for amusement; and then getting so built round, tho' the fine Surrey commons are at the back.

We had tea. Collins told me some curious particulars about the Princess's marriage. The Emperor wouldn't hear of her marrying into his circle, for fear of *health* reasons and delicacy. When Collins suggested Teck to the Princess she said artlessly 'Oh, that would be very nice'. And it seems a great success.

The Princess talked with immense enthusiasm of Churton Collins and the stimulus of his literary lectures; I should like to talk about literature with her; and Miss Potts tried to start it, but it wouldn't do and we went off in jests. After tea we sate an *immense* time – two hours – talking and joking – a flood of absurd stories. Oh, how tired I got!! Only one story remains with me. Raper said that when one of seven brothers died by an accident and the vicar had to break it to the eldest, a sensitive delicate man, the vicar had only just said 'I am sorry to say your brother has had a fatal accident', the man cried out 'Oh, let me guess which', a kind of frightful nervousness, I suppose.

The Duchess related a horrible experience of seeing Albany fidgeting with one of his eyes. She called him, and saw a little green speck like a leaf; she got hold of it, and drew out a long white thread, which turned her quite faint. It was only a stalk of cress, but she thought she had pulled out some nerve.

We got away at 7.0 and I went and slept; woke refreshed. Dined at 8.0. The horror of seeing so much of the same people rather grows on me. I took in the Princess, told her stories, made her laugh. She said at last 'Well, it is very nice; but here have we been doing nothing ever since lunch but talking and laughing – and Sunday too!' I said, 'But it is also Xmas day, and that excuses anything.'

Then in the drawing-room we played a funny game, jerking,

with a spring made like a hand, little paper cones like extinguishers into a sort of net. It sounds stupid, but Raper's performances were incredibly funny. He never knew how to do it, but sent his cones flying all over the place, into peoples' hair and eyes – very goodhumoured over it. Then we went and smoked, and here came in one of those horrible little bits of etiquette. The Prince didn't sit down; so nobody else did; and we stood for an hour. I was half-dead with fatigue and strangled yawns. It was stupid of him; but I suppose he thought everyone would sit if they wanted.

I forgot to say that the Duchess talking of the Prince Consort said that he was so ill-tempered with his children – beating and even kicking them! The blameless Arthurian Prince!

They have at last fitted up the Queen's rooms for use and the Tecks have them.

Monday, December 26. I slept well; and woke light-hearted. Breakfast; I like the old clock on the stairs which at certain hours plays a sweet old Handelian minuet on flutes. It woke me last night and I lay and listened softly.

Raper told me, what I didn't know, that Uncle Arthur [Sidgwick] was practically offered the Presidentship of Corpus. The undergraduates petitioned for him. They asked if he would attend chapel, and he said he could give no sort of pledge. Then they gave up. But the meeting which selected Case was held at his house. I think we are the kind of people who don't get things. He seems, I hear from M.B., quite content; he did not wish to drop his political work. He is an odd creature – very childlike in many ways; has never, I think, *quite* grown up.

I left all my things in my room; and drove off, after warm goodbyes, to the station. I feel very gratefully and cordially towards these good people, and have really advanced in intimacy with them. The Duchess, talking of my stories, *Isles of Sunset*, said to me 'I must be frank. I like most of them; but "Out of the Sea" is simply horrid; it shows one nothing: I can't think how you can have written it. There! That is off my mind.' Her German accent varies very much – sometimes she is really difficult to understand; but she talks very racy English. . . .

... *Thursday, December 29.* Lunched in haste and caught train to Esher; the country pretty, but I was now overshadowed. Was met by a trap, and driving up found the Duchess and my little Duke by the steps. Both very warm in greetings. He looks very nice, very well and a little manlier. Then certain gentlemen in waiting drifted up – Collins etc. The little Duke took me to my room and stayed long talking about his military duties which seem to interest him but weigh on him. He has to instruct 76 men in the duties of a soldier, loyalty, obedience etc. Then they are inspected and the Emperor asks all kinds of inconsequent questions 'Who is the Pope?'; 'Who is the Sultan?' – a recruit says: 'A dog, your Majesty', or 'a man with many wives'. He doesn't mind, as long as *some* answer is made. If they are dumb, he abuses the officers. Or he will say 'Arrest me the Field-Marshal' to see if the recruit knows what to do. After the arrest, he will say 'Now run, Marshal!' Then he says to the recruit, 'Now, do your duty.' The recruit has to warn him and then fire. Albany says that you can't escape censure. This is rather striking. He then described his own guards and the horrible march past. But it is all very good for him.

Then I inscribed my little presents; went down to tea in hall – a large vague party, but all pleasant. Then we went to the saloon; all servants and hands, indoors and out, trooped in and we sang 'Hark the Herald', played very nervously by the Princess. Then into the Dining-room. A huge Xmas Tree, tables covered with gifts. The servants all called up, and presents made, the Duchess giving each. Miss Potts says she is so shy, she *can't* talk to them in their own houses, but her kindness is amazing. Then the guests; and I was *loaded* with treasures – photos, a silver ash-tray from the Prince and Princess, a gold cup from the Duchess, a book, a photo and calendar from the Duke etc. There was a really magnificent show of presents. The whole festival really very nice. Then we strolled about; and I unfortunately backed into the tree and set my nice coat on fire, diffusing a horrible smell of burnt cloth. Much laughter and commiseration – a punishment for having no frock-coat! Or a providence? Since when I have been in my room, reading and writing quietly. ... The clock outside strikes up its sweet little minuet. That is good!

Dinner was very late – 8.30 – and in the front hall, on the billiard table, as the dining-room was laden with gifts. The glare of the lamps, the low chairs distressing. The little Duke very smart in his garter. He has two men with him, Eckhardt, an accomplished, rather effeminate man, who suffers himself to be feebly ragged by the Duke, and a man like a white duck, a Prussian sprig, who is – I believe – a friend. He can't talk any known language, so we can only nod and smile.

Raper, one side of me at dinner, uttering oracles; he had read all my poems – *Lord Vyet* – which I had given him, and discoursed. The Duke the other side of me. I was pleased to see how ascetic he is – ate very little except soup, fish, and some vegetables; drank water, and half a glass of champagne. Does not smoke. Perhaps he gets his clear porcelain look from this. But he looks older and manlier, and has more of a moustache. He was silent at first, but soon launched out about the student corps and his duel. It is a narrow little mind, I think; intensely preoccupied with the Students' Club, and the colours worn. But the duel did him credit. Princes are forbidden to fight (as being officers). If they ever do, some incapable fencer is chosen. But Albany fought a man who had fought ten duels; failed to wound him, but got a slash on the forehead himself and a great cut in the scalp. The scar doesn't show. The great point is never to *wince* – any wound is at once probed by a surgeon, and that he found sickening. But he got through all right – though he confessed that he lay awake all the night before – and it has evidently brought him considerable popularity and credit. He is obviously very proud of it all; gave me a photo of himself in the absurd student club uniform, which he thinks very grand. His little diplomacy came out in this; he gave me one of the *cartes;* but next day in his room we came upon a heap of them in *cabinet.* He felt bound to offer me one of the larger ones, and was relieved when I retained the carte.

The Emperor was furious at the time – but Albany has since discovered that he was rather pleased. This shows a pleasant streak of ambition and physical daring in the boy. But he does not seem to be interested in anything much except his military duties. His vitality is evidently not great. He has curious little obstinacies of mind. He goes to Sandringham tomorrow. He said he would go in a frock-coat. They assured him it was unnecessary; but he stuck to it and appeared at breakfast in it. Then Collins said 'Everyone else will be in short coats. You will only feel ridiculous.' Albany maintained with an odd rather sullen look that it was the right thing to wear – but presently went away and changed it.

After dinner the lieutenant played. I murmured with Raper about agreeable subjects such as the immortality of the soul. Then some of them danced. I cannot help liking and admiring the gaiety and unaffected cheerfulness of Collins. He was seen dancing a jig in a corner by himself – and then danced with anyone he could get. I complimented him on his spirits (he is 64). 'Anything to keep things going!' he said. He is a truly delightful man – wise, intelligent, and yet as simple as a child. I don't know what the Duchess would do without him. He is always cheerful, respectful, observant, kind. His friendship is the best thing I have got out of my connection with Claremont. His white stiff hair, sanguine complexion, half-shut eyes, mobile lips make him look like an old priest; and there is a modesty and sweetness about him that I envy with all my heart.

In the library followed one of those *hideous* standing performances. For over an hour we *stood* and smoked. I was nearly dead with fatigue and boredom.

Friday, December 30. After a good night, got down to breakfast a little late – still in the front hall. Then Miss Potts and Raper went off. I had a little talk with Raper and found that he had *twice* refused the Mastership of Trinity, Oxford – and a D.C.L. This interests me. I asked him why. 'Oh', he said, 'it's not my line – I hate decorations; and I hate responsibility. I could not have borne it.' In these days when promotion comes from all the four corners of the earth, this was rather refreshing.

I was glad to have seen something of this wise and good man. He told me a curious instance of *Providence*. A site in the Malvern Hills, which he had always thought the most beautiful in England, offered him for £600. But he did not buy it, which rather does for Providence!

Then I went to Albany's room – a pleasant sunny place – hung with watercolours, and had an odd dumb-show talk with the Prussian. Then we went all over the gardens, farm etc. The whole place is kept *down*, everything being originally on rather a grand scale. We saw the great bull and plenty of pigs and cows, a dairy etc. The gardens very pleasant. The wind was tremendous. I was glad to find Albany so anxious for exercise. And he was nice and courteous to all the people. He looked very English, except his long pointed boots. But he evidently talks German better than English now and has an accent.

We had an early lunch, and then he, Collins and the two suite went off to town. He said a very affectionate goodbye to me, over and over, adding to my dismay 'I shall expect you at Coburg in July when I come of age.' This is a terrible prospect.

Then we sate and talked and drank coffee. Then a long slow walk, through the beautiful pinewoods, I acting equerry, with keys. We visited a disused well-house, where a tramp had lately encamped for weeks; and to a beautiful pool, fringed with tall sedge – such a lovely colour, in the middle of the woods. The Duchess entertained me with very humorous stories of small German courts, especially the Count of Erbach, living in a filthy and ruinous house, no money, but always driving four-in-hand and refusing to see any but the nobility. 'Blood-royal' is the one thought, and to keep the blood pure. 'There is no such snobbishness in the world', she said, 'as at small German courts.' She told me how the Prince of Saxe-Weimar would not take in Princess Marie of Baden to dinner because she married the Duke of Hamilton. 'I can't go in with an English Duchess', he said pathetically. Later in the evening he offered the Duchess of Albany his arm. 'I thought you said you could not go in with an English Duchess', she said. He was very angry.

This walk amused and interested me. The Princess was so gay and bright, the whole thing so homely and quiet. It seems that Teck said to the Duchess this morning 'You are losing all your old friends and making no new ones.' 'There's Mr Benson', she said. 'Oh well, he will do', said Teck frankly, 'but you must get him to bring you some new people.' I see that very few people come here from the Visitors' Book. They evidently live a *very* quiet life, though the Duchess goes about a good deal. She is a very shy straightforward woman, and hates unfamiliar things. But once make a friend of her, and she does not forget. She is now very maternal with me. When she asked me to come a walk, I said feebly 'if I am not in the way'. She said smartly 'Now do not begin these *discretions* – they are so disagreeable.' Lady Collins laughed and said 'Now you have got it.' They have a funny way of calling you simply by your surname. 'Benson, sit here – Raper, sit there', the Duchess says.

We were in about four. Then came tea and Teck returned. Princess Alice scrambling through Xmas letters. A curious talk about the Queen. The Duchess said that for an outspoken strong-willed person, she was fearfully shy – could not be criticised; and was never at ease with a *man*. Curiously undecided about small things, could not make up her mind where to breakfast, where to drive to – and it was thus that John Brown got his influence over her, by making up her mind for her. She spent most of her day in writing letters, preferring to write even to her Private Secretary when in the house. Princess Henry's marriage revealed to her that she really enjoyed society still.

Then we all dispersed; I went off, wrote a few letters and diary. I am glad I stayed today, because I think I have really made more of a friend of the Duchess. I never saw a person more sincerely anxious to do good and to be good. She amused me by telling me that she implored Albany to avoid *pomp*. 'Make your house like a private gentleman's', she said, 'everything nice, but simple – like Sandringham.'

At Claremont with the Duchess of Albany

At 8.0 we assembled for dinner. One of the few things that makes me absolutely furious is the way in which all these Royalties take each other in to dinner and sit next each other. The Duchess was talking today with scorn of the little German royalties who are poor and poky, but yet feel that they may marry sovereigns. 'Royal blood is the only thing that matters', she said. 'It makes them different from all the world, with a line round them.' But I expect that the Duchess suffers too from the disease, and none the less because she thinks that she has got rid of it all. What else would excuse being taken in by your son-in-law night after night, or sending your son and daughter arm-in-arm into dinner *first*. A boy and girl of 20 and 21 ! Then this absurd Calenberg (or whatever his name is) because he is a Count, has to be sent in first etc. If this is not snobbery, what is? However I sat between the Princess and Lady Collins tonight; so had no cause to complain. The Princess was very lively, like a bird, flying about from one thing to another. Lady Collins engaged in a long argument with me on matrimony. She said, 'a man before he engages himself ought to ask some other woman, a friend of his object, what she is really like. He is bound to be in a mist about her. He can't tell whether she will make a *comrade.*'

I said 'But would any woman ever advise any man not to marry? I thought they were all matchmakers at heart.' This remark fell loudly into a still pool of thought. Lady Collins looked at me reprovingly and said 'Ah, you don't know.' Collins looked at me fixedly. I said 'What is the matter?' Collins said 'Well, I am so stupefied by your last remark, that I am trying to arrange my thoughts.' Then followed laughter. But the Duchess looked at me and shook her head.

We sipped wine; and I talked to Teck on commonplace subjects of perennial interest, and told him the tale of Harry Milner at Leicester and Walter Durnford at Syracuse. Then to play Bridge. A *very* slow game. The Princess cried out at last 'How slow this is!' I said 'I hope you mean only in respect of the time it occupies?' The Duchess said 'Now I see where all the fine speeches in your books come from.'

At Claremont with the Duchess of Albany

Then we smoked; and were allowed to sit down. Teck talked in broken German to Calenberg. A good night; woke, but with a peaceful mind.

Saturday, December 31. Breakfast at 9.0. The Duchess very warm and kind. She pointed to the place by her and said 'Now just sit down there and let us have a talk. It is very good of your mother to have allowed you to be with us all this time, but I am not sorry I insisted, not a bit repentant. I wanted you to see our German Xmas and to see Charlie, and to be one of us', and she gave me a great kind jolly smile. Then I made some pretty speeches.

After that I had to write my name. I find it is my fifth visit here. Then the Duchess took me to her room, and I talked with her and the Princess about the Coburg arrangement, till I had to go. It seems that the boy has about 34 manorhouses and castles. But he will live in two castles at Coburg and two at Gotha. He has to live 100 days in each. Then he has a huge *Austrian* estate – so big that he had no less than 37 livings in his gift, village churches all in the estate. Duke Alfred never went there; it might be very profitable, but it only just pays its way. Then he has a Prussian estate, at Posen, dating from the time when Duke Ernst wanted to be Emperor, and a shooting-box in the Tyrol. There are, I suppose, the materials for happiness here. But I would not take it as a gift. There must be *incessant* fuss, pomp, bother, social duties: indeed, I can't conceive a more utterly *tiresome* life.

Then she told me all about his Court officials – secretaries etc. Then I had to go; and I got a very warm goodbye from both the ladies; and the servants were friendly too, tho' they have lost my umbrella between them. . . .

Before I consider the year that is over, let me say a few words about Claremont. I have enjoyed it as an experience; and I have admired the good sense, kindliness and simplicity of the three, Duchess, Princess and Prince. But of course Collins is the pivot of the whole thing, though they don't know it. His courtesy, patience, devotion, gaiety, geniality make him the real centre of the house. The others all show very commonplace beside him.

At Claremont with the Duchess of Albany

I admire him all the more because I *couldn't* live in that atmosphere of false deference and elaborate ceremony. I can't really breathe there. I am never anything but *on a visit*. I could no more sit down and write my book there than I could fly. It isn't my *monde* at all, and it is too late to begin.

[Volume 63, pp.45–78; Volume 64, pp.1–9]

Index

Index

Index

Index

Index

Index

Index

Index